EP Math 1

Parent's Guide

THIRD EDITION

Welcome to the EP Math 1 Parent's Guide!

This little book was created to help you go offline while following EP's Math 1 curriculum. You will need the Math 1 student workbook for your child. Without the online lessons, you will need to be your child's teacher. The directions are here for introducing new topics. The workbook will provide practice and review.

This book also includes objectives for each day, materials marked where needed, directions for what to do each day, and the complete answer key.

Some of the pages have directions to color in something just for fun. On those days I marked crayons as optional. They aren't needed for completing the lesson, but there is a use for them if you want. I only did this because you may be schooling on the run, and you don't need to make sure to bring crayons if it's not really needed to complete the lesson. I'm just trying to help you out and make things as easy as I can!

And a little note: To avoid calling all children "he" or the awkward phrasing of "him or her," I've used the plural pronoun when referring to your child, such as, "Show the clock to your child and have them point to the hour hand."

Have a great year.

Lee

Odd and Even

Day 1 (crayons)

- Students will: count to 20.
- Day 1 worksheet

Day 2

- Students will: count to 100.
- Day 2 worksheet
- Quiz your child asking what number comes before or after a given number. eg. "What number comes after 23?"

Day 3 (crayon, blocks or other small item)

- Students will: learn odd and even.
- Introduce the terms odd and even. Take a small number of items (blocks work well) and divide them into two even groups. Explain that an even number of items can be divided evenly. Each item will have a pair. Take one away and explain that an odd number of items cannot. There's one left over.
- Day 3 worksheet
- Have your child color the odd numbers from the first row of the chart. Show your child how every number below them ends in the same number, which also makes them odd numbers.

Day 4 (crayon – different color than Day 3)

- Students will: review odd and even.
- Day 4 worksheet

Day 5

- Students will: review odd and even, develop memory skills.
- Day 5 worksheet
- Play a memory game together. "I went to the store and bought apples." The next person says, "I went to the store and bought apples and bananas." You continue adding new foods and remembering what came before for as long as you can.
  - Each new item you "buy" should start with the next letter in the alphabet. That way you can use the order of the alphabet to prompt your memory for what food comes next.

Writing numbers 1 – 100, Patterns

Day 6

- Students will: identify patterns, skip count by twos, review counting and odd numbers.
- Day 6+ worksheet, 100 Square Chart, Follow the instructions for Day 6, writing in the numbers up through 20. Then have your child point to number 1 and read it out loud, and then jump to 3 and say it out loud. Have your child continue to skip count by two, reading aloud all of the odd numbers up to 19.
- Day 6 worksheet, Help your child see the first pattern.

Day 7

- Students will: identify patterns, skip count by two, review even numbers.
- Day 6+ worksheet, 100 Square Chart, Follow the instructions for Day 7, writing in the numbers from 21 - 40. Then have your child point to number 22 and read it out loud, and then jump to 24 and say it out loud. Have your child continue to skip count by two, reading aloud all of the even numbers up to 40.
- Day 7 worksheet, Help your child see the first pattern.

Day 8

- Students will: identify patterns, skip count by two, review odd numbers.
- Day 6+ worksheet, 100 Square Chart, Follow the instructions for Day 8, writing in the numbers from 41 - 60.
- Have your child try to skip count by two from 41 to 59 without looking at the paper. You will be saying only the odd numbers.
- Day 8 worksheet, Help your child see the first pattern.

Day 9

- Students will: skip count by two, review even numbers.
- Day 6+ worksheet, 100 Square Chart, Follow the instructions for Day 9, writing in the numbers from 61 - 80.
- Have your child try to skip count by two from 62 to 80 without looking at the paper. You will be saying only the even numbers.
- Day 9 worksheet, Help your child get started showing how to use skip counting to fill in the blanks.

Day 10

- Students will: write numbers up to 100, count backward, skip count by two, practice odd numbers.
- Day 6+ worksheet, 100 Square Chart, Follow the instructions for Day 10, writing in the numbers from 91 - 100.
- Have your child try to count backward from 100.
- Day 10 worksheet, Help your child get started, showing how to use skip counting to fill in the blanks. The second part is not just skip counting by two. They need to look for a pattern. At the bottom of the page, they need to put the numbers in order from smallest to largest. If they are ever unsure of an exercise like this or get it wrong, look together at the hundreds chart to see which number comes first on the chart.

Number Words, Ordinals

Day 11

- Students will: count with ordinal numbers, write numbers from words, write words from numbers.
- Count with your child up to ten using ordinal numbers: first, second, third, fourth, fifth, sixth, seventh, eighth, ninth, tenth.
- Day 11 worksheet

Day 12 (toy cars or any object for a race)

- Students will: count with ordinal numbers, read and write ordinal numbers with digits and letters up to ten.
- Play a race game with your child. Maybe use toy cars or figures and have them race. Have your child say who came in first, second, third, and fourth.
- Ask your child what is the first letter of the alphabet. Ask your child what is the second letter of the alphabet. Continue through the sixth letter (F).
- Day 12 worksheet
  - They can see how to write ordinals (such as 1st) by looking at the numbers on the bottom of the page.

Day 13 (crayon)

- Students will: practice following directions, use ordinal numbers, read and write numbers from eleven to twenty with digits and letters.
- Day 13 worksheet

Day 14

- Students will: read and write numbers from twenty-one to thirty with digits and letters.
- Day 14 worksheet

Day 15

- Students will: practice skip counting by twos, read and write numbers counting by tens to one hundred with digits and letters, develop memory skills.
- Have your child start at two and count by twos to twenty.
- Day 15 worksheet
- Play a memory game. "I went to the zoo, and I saw an alligator." The next person continues naming an animal that begins with B but also repeats the first animal. If you get stuck, use adjectives – a Quiet moose.

Adding 0 and 1

Day 16 (five coins, can use something else)

- Students will: be introduced to the concept of adding zero.
- Day 16 worksheet, You will do the first activity with your child. Go through the motion of handing over zero coins.

Day 17 (5 blocks, can use something else)

- Students will: be introduced to the concept of adding one.
- Day 17 worksheet
- You could quiz your child on adding one, even doing bigger numbers like "What's 52 plus 1?"

Day 18

- Students will: practice with adding one.
- Have your child write 3 + 1 = 4 on a piece of paper and then draw a picture of that problem. Think about stacking and counting from day 17.
- Day 18 worksheet

Day 19 (eleven pieces of scrap paper)

- Students will: learn to use a number line.
- Get 11 pieces of scrap paper. Computer paper used on one side would be perfect.
  - Write a number big on each piece of paper from 0 to 10.
  - Lay the papers out in order. This is a number line.
  - Have your child stand on zero. Have your child add one, take one step and stand on the answer, and say, "Zero plus 1 equals 1."
  - Have your child add one again, stand on the answer, say, "1 + 1 = 2"
  - Keep doing the same until you get to ten.
- Day 19 worksheet
- Let your child play with the timeline. What's 0 + 10? Start on zero and take ten steps to get to the answer. You can decide if you want to hang onto these to use/play with in the future. I give it as an option on Day 29.

Day 20

- Students will: practice adding one and zero.
- Have your child draw a picture of a math problem adding zero or one and then write the equation for the picture.
- Day 20 worksheet, They need to pay attention that this time they are to put the biggest number first and the smallest number last
- Play a memory game. "I went to the park and I saw an apple tree." Keep going, adding things that you saw at the park (noun practice!). Each one should start with the next letter of the alphabet. That's what helps you remember them in order. The first letter is a hook to hang the memory on to help prompt remembering the word.

Addition

Day 21

- Students will: use a number line to add.
- Day 21 worksheet, Check to make sure your child isn't counting the starting number. You place your finger on the first number and then count as you jump forward.

Day 22 (up to ten small objects for counting/adding)

- Students will: count objects to add.
- Have your child bring you some small objects (fewer than ten). Put them into two groups. Have your child count how many are in each group. Have your child count how many there are all together.
- Day 22 worksheet
- Ask your child to draw a picture of 2 + 3 = 5.

Day 23

- Students will: practice adding with one and zero, answer vertical addition problems by counting to add.
- Day 23 worksheet

Day 24

- Students will: learn the math fact $2 + 2 = 4$, practice addition with known facts.
- On the math facts check list in the beginning of the book, check off that your child has learned $2 + 2 = 4$. Use this when you are supposed to quiz your child. It will help you remember which facts they know so far to quiz them on. You could also start a list to hang in the house or write each new fact on an index card to make your flashcards with the facts they know so far.
  - Today's fact is $2 + 2 = 4$.
  - Tell your child and quiz your child, "What's two plus two?"
  - You can ask your child throughout the day even.
- Day 24 worksheet

Day 25

- Students will: learn the math fact $2 + 3 = 5$, practice addition with known facts.
- Do this addition concept comprehension activity with your child.
  - Now I want you to look at your left hand. How many fingers are on it? 5, right?
  - Now, hold three of your fingers together with your right hand. You have two fingers free and three fingers being held. That's two plus three equals five.
  - Now, hold onto just two fingers. You have three fingers free and two fingers being held. That's three plus two.
  - So what does $3 + 2 = ?$ 5! You still have five fingers! It doesn't matter which way you hold them.
  - So, we learned that $2 + 3 = 5$ AND $3 + 2 = 5$.
- Add these to your facts list. (Check them off and if you are doing anything else, add both of these facts.)
- Day 25 worksheet
- Play a memory game. "I packed for vacation and put in my suitcase one guitar." This time instead of using the letters of the alphabet, each time take one more of something. "I packed for vacation and put in my suitcase one guitar and two pairs of sneakers."

Day 26

- Students will: learn the math fact $3 + 3 = 6$, practice addition with known facts.
- Add $3 + 3 = 6$ to your facts list.

- Quiz your child. Make sure to have your child say the whole problem out loud, "Three plus three equals six."
- Day 26 worksheet

Day 27 (six coins, can use something else)

- Students will: learn the math fact $2 + 4 = 6$, practice addition with known facts.
- Do this addition concept comprehension activity with your child.
  - Get out six coins (or you could use something else). Put them all together in a pile. That's $6 + 0$. Six coins plus no more coins.
  - Move one coin off all by itself. That's 5 coins plus 1 coin. You still have six coins, right? $5 + 1 = 6$.
    - And, if you look at it the other way, it's $1 + 5 = 6$.
  - Now move another coin to be with the one coin. How many coins are in each pile?
    - Now you have a pile of 4 coins and a pile of 2 coins. That's $4 + 2 = 6$.
    - If you look at it the other way it's $2 + 4 = 6$.
  - Move one more coin so they both have three coins. That's $3 + 3 = 6$.
  - Ask your child to see how there is always the same number of coins. The answer is always 6. But there are lots of ways to get that answer because you can move the coins into different combinations.
- Add to your math facts list: $2 + 4 = 6$ and $4 + 2 = 6$.
- Make sure to have your child say the problem out loud, "Two plus four equals six. Four plus two equals six."
- Day 27 worksheet

Day 28

- Students will: learn the math fact $3 + 4 = 7$, practice addition with known facts.
- Have your child draw the problem $3 + 4 = 7$.
- Add this to your facts list.
- Make sure to have your child say the problem out loud, "Three plus four equals seven. Four plus three equals seven." $3 + 4 = 7$ and $4 + 3 = 7$
  - If your child really likes to draw, you could have your child draw a picture of each math fact. If your child really likes these, you could save them in a binder for review or hang them on the wall.
- Day 28 worksheet

Day 29 (number line papers if you saved them)

- Students will: learn the math fact 4 + 4 = 8, practice addition with known facts.
- Either get out your number papers and line them up on the floor, or use the number line in your workbook on Day 21.
  - Have your child find 4 and either stand on it or put their finger on it.
  - Now have your child move four more, and ask what number they landed on.
- Add 4 + 4 = 8 to your math facts.
- Quiz your child. Make sure your child says out loud, "Four plus four equals eight."
- Day 29 worksheet

Day 30

- Students will: practice with known facts, including filling in missing numbers. Students will develop memory muscles.
- Day 30 worksheet, Don't let them get stuck on part B. Let it be a fun puzzle to solve. They can use part A to help them figure out most of the answers. Tell them they are exercising their brains, making them stronger.
- Play a memory game. "I went to the park and I ate." Keep adding a new action verb. "I went to the park and I ate and biked." "I went to the park and I ate, biked, and crawled." Go as far as you can.

Counting (backward, by ten)

Day 31

- Students will: count backward, practice with known addition facts.
- Quiz your child from your math facts sheet. Make sure to ask questions both ways. eg. 2 + 4 and 4 + 2
- Day 31 worksheet

Day 32 (Legos/Duplos, try to have at least 30 of whatever you use)

- Students will: count by tens forward and backward, learn the math fact 2 + 5 = 7, practice addition with known facts.
- Get out a whole bunch of Legos or coins, or whatever you decide to use.
  - Make stacks or rows of ten. (Make up to three stacks. It's okay if you don't have that many, though.)
  - Put away any extras.
  - One stack (or row) is made up of ten.
  - How many are in two stacks (or rows)?
    - 20
    - If your child isn't sure, go ahead and count them all together.
    - (Continued on the next page....)

- o How many are in three stacks (or rows)?
  - ▪ 30
- o Ask your child how many would be in four stacks (rows) of ten?
  - ▪ 40
- o Ask your child how many would be in five stacks (rows) of ten?
  - ▪ 50
- o Count together from 10 to 50 by tens. Then count backward from 50 by tens.
- Add to your facts list 2 + 5 = 7 and 5 + 2 = 7.
- Have your child say the new fact out loud and quiz your child with these facts and a few others.
- Day 32 worksheet

Day 33

- Students will: count by ten, learn the math fact 3 + 5 = 8, practice addition with known facts.
- Count by tens to one hundred. Count backward from one hundred by tens.
- Add 3 + 5 = 8 and 5 + 3 = 8 to your facts list.
- Have your child say these new facts out loud.
- Day 33 worksheet

Day 34

- Students will: count by tens forward and backward, learn the math fact 4 + 5 = 9, practice addition with known facts.
- Have your child count on their own by tens up to 100 and back down again.
- Add 4 + 5 = 9 and 5 + 4 = 9 to your facts list.
- Day 34 worksheet

Day 35

- Students will: learn the math fact 5 + 5 = 10, practice addition with known facts, solve missing number problems.
- Have your child look at their two hands, holding them out in front of themselves.
  - o You have five fingers on your left hand and five fingers on your right hand. That's five plus five fingers.
  - o How many fingers do you have in all? 10! Say, 'Five plus five equals ten.'
- Add 5 + 5 = 10 to your facts list.
- Day 35 worksheet, Don't let your child get bogged down on the missing numbers. Encourage them to use what they know. If they can't think, "What plus five equals eight?" for example, have them make a guess. "Does two plus five equal eight? No, two plus five is seven. Eight is bigger than seven; that wasn't big enough. Pick a bigger number to try," etc. Make it a challenge to conquer. Celebrate their accomplishment.

Addition Practice

Day 36

- Students will: practice with known addition facts.
- Day 36 worksheet, Depending on how well the worksheet is going, you can decide if your child would benefit from you quizzing them on their facts.

Day 37

- Students will: practice with known addition facts.
- Day 37 worksheet

Day 38

- Students will: practice with known addition facts.
- Day 38 worksheet

Day 39

- Students will: practice with known addition facts.
- Day 39 worksheet

Day 40

- Students will: practice with known addition facts.
- Day 40 worksheet
- Cheer for your child learning these addition facts.

Addition and Review

Day 41 (optional: six chocolate chips)

- Students will: review odd and even, practice known addition facts.
- Remind your child about odd and even.
  - An even number of objects can be divided into two groups.
  - If you want to have some fun, give your child six chocolate chips to divide evenly between the two of you.
  - Even numbers are 2, 4, 6, 8, 10.
  - Odd numbers are 1, 3, 5, 7, 9.
  - Even numbers are 22, 24, 26, 28, 30.
  - Odd numbers are 41, 43, 45, 47, 49.
  - (Continued on the next page…)

10

- What matters is the last number. Two million one is an odd number because it ends with a one.
    - Is three million eight an odd or even number?
- Day 41 worksheet

Day 42

- Students will: practice with odd and even, practice known facts.
- Quiz your child on the addition facts they have learned.
- Day 42 worksheet

Day 43

- Students will: practice counting, ordinals, and addition.
- Day 43 worksheet

Day 44

- Students will: practice counting, ordinals, and addition.
- Day 44 worksheet

Day 45 (crayon)

- Students will: count by ten, count backward, write number words.
- Day 45 worksheet
- Here's a game that you can play with your child any time you are sitting at the table together. Have your child put their hand flat on the table and put one object at the end of each finger. While your child closes their eyes, take away any number of them, and have your child open their eyes and tell how many are in your hand.

Patterns, Addition Practice

Day 46

- Students will find patterns and practice addition facts.
- Day 46+ worksheet, Have your child just do the top row.
- Day 46 worksheet

Day 47

- Students will find patterns and practice addition facts.
- Day 46+ worksheet, Have your child just do the next row.
- Day 47 worksheet

Day 48

- Students will find patterns and practice addition facts.
- Day 46+ worksheet, Have your child just do the next row.
- Day 48 worksheet

Day 49

- Students will find patterns and practice addition facts.
- Day 46+ worksheet, Have your child just do the next row.
- Day 49 worksheet

Day 50

- Students will find patterns and practice addition facts.
- Day 46+ worksheet, Have your child just do the next row.
- Day 50 worksheet

Comparing Numbers

Day 51

- Students will: identify greater and lesser numbers, practice addition facts.
- Day 51+ worksheet, Have your child just do the first row.
- Day 51 worksheet, They can also think of which number comes first in counting.

Day 52

- Students will: use greater than and less than symbols, practice addition facts.
- Show your child 1 < 2.
  - This symbol, which looks like an open alligator mouth, means that two is greater than one.
  - You can write it like this too.
    - 2 > 1
- The big open side of the symbol opens to the big number.
- The little pointy side points to the littler number.
- Tear off the greater than/less than symbol from this page or draw it on another little piece of paper. Have your child place it in the examples on the following page.
  - 4 < 9
  - 50 < 75
  - 31 > 15
  - Make sure they point the big end to the big number and the small end to the small number.

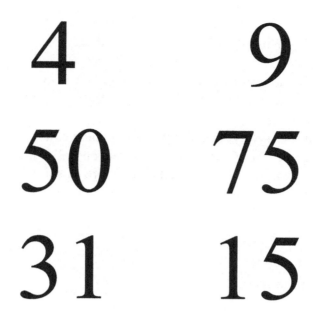

- Day 52 worksheet
- Day 51+ worksheet, Have your child just do the next row.

Day 53

- Students will: use greater than and less than symbols, practice addition facts.
- Remind your child how to write the greater than/less than symbol and that the big end points to the bigger number and the little end points to the smaller number.
- Day 53 worksheet
- Day 51+ worksheet, Have your child just do the next row.
- Quiz your child on math facts from your list.

Day 54

- Students will: use greater than and less than symbols, practice addition facts.
- Remind your child how to write the greater than/less than symbol and that the big end points to the bigger number and the little end points to the smaller number.
- Day 54 worksheet
- Day 51+ worksheet, Have your child just do the next row.
- Quiz your child on math facts from your list.

Day 55

- Students will: use greater than and less than symbols, practice addition facts, build memory muscle.
- Remind your child how to write the greater than/less than symbol and that the big end points to the bigger number and the little end points to the smaller number.
- Day 55 worksheet
- Day 51+ worksheet, Have your child just do the next row.
- Play a memory game "For Christmas I want one chair." This time instead of using the letters of the alphabet, each time take one more of something. "For Christmas I want one chair and two cakes."

Measurements

Day 56 (ruler with centimeters)

- Students will: measure in centimeters, practice addition facts.
- Get out a ruler. (You can print one from online.)
  - Show your child how to use it to measure in centimeters.
  - Have your child try to find something that is 10 centimeters long (or other number if that proves difficult).
- Day 56 worksheet
- Day 56+ worksheet, Have your child just do the first row.

Day 57 (ruler with inches)

- Students will: measure in inches, practice addition facts.
- Get out a ruler that can measure inches. (You can print one from online.)
  - Show your child how to use it to measure in inches. They will just be measuring to whole inches.
  - Have your child try to find something that is four inches long (or another number if that proves difficult).
- Day 57 worksheet
- Day 56+ worksheet, Have your child just do the next row.

Day 58 (crayon, book)

- Students will: measure in generic units, practice addition facts.
- Get out a book and measure your child with it. Tell your child how many books tall they are.
- Have your child measure the couch or table with the book.
- Day 58 worksheet
- Day 56+ worksheet, Have your child just do the next row.

Day 59 (inch ruler)

- Students will: practice addition facts, learn the relative size of inches, feet, yards, and miles.
- Get out your inch ruler. Have your child show you how big one inch is.
- Ask your child how long twelve inches is.
  - That's probably the whole ruler, one foot.
- Ask your child if you would measure the length of your finger with inches or feet.
  - inches, It's less than a foot.
- Ask your child if you would measure the height of a window in inches or feet.
  - feet, You could measure in inches, but feet would be simpler.
- Tell your child that a yard is three feet. Have your child measure out three feet, marking the beginning and the end, to show the size of a yard.
- Ask your child what they might measure in yards instead of feet or inches.
  - the yard, the driveway, the height of your house, etc.
- Tell your child that a mile is 5,280 feet.
- Ask your child what they might measure in miles.
  - Miles are used for measuring distances, like how far it is to the store.
- Day 59 worksheet
- Day 56+ worksheet, Have your child do the next row.

Day 60

- Students will practice addition facts and complete a number maze.
- Day 56+ worksheet, Have your child do the last row.
- Day 60 worksheet

Day 61

- Students will practice addition including solving for missing numbers.
- Day 61+ worksheet, Have your child do the first row.
- Day 61 worksheet

Day 62 (glass thermometer if available, otherwise will use the workbook picture)

- Students will practice addition facts and learn to read a thermometer.
- You will be introducing your child to reading a thermometer. If you have a glass one, go get it to look at together.
  - If you don't have a thermometer, just open to the Day 62 workbook page and look at those pictures.
  - Things to talk about.
    - A thermometer tells us the temperature.
    - If we hang a thermometer outside, it tells us the temperature outside. If we have one inside, it tells us the temperature of that room. (This lesson is continued on the next page.)

- A hot temperature is up high on the thermometer. A cold temperature is down low on a thermometer.
    - We read a thermometer by seeing how high it fills up. The temperature is the number by the top of the line that fills inside the thermometer.
    - Take a look at a thermometer (or the pictures in the workbook) and show your child how to see where the line is and what the temperature is.
        - Ask your child what they think the thermometer would say if it were in a hot desert?
        - What about in Antarctica?
        - Where is today's temperature about on a thermometer?
- Day 62 worksheet, You may need to help your child figure out the few that don't have a number next to the top of the line.
- Day 61+ worksheet, Have your child do the next row.

Day 63 (red crayon)

- Students will practice addition facts and reading thermometers.
- Day 61+ worksheet, Have your child do the next row.
- Day 63 worksheet

Day 64

- Students will practice addition facts and estimate weights.
- Day 61+ worksheet, Have your child do the next row.
- Day 64 worksheet
- Quiz your child on the addition facts from your sheet to make sure they are all known.

Day 65

- Students will: practice addition facts, find patterns, build memory muscle.
- Day 61+ worksheet, Have your child do the last row.
- Day 65 worksheet
- Play a memory game. This time make a sound song. The first person makes a sound. It can be any kind of sound such as a bark, a click, a tap, a clap, a snarf, a note, etc. The next person does the same one and then adds one. How far can you get?

Review

Day 66

- Students will: practice addition facts, find the greater and lesser numbers, review the greater than/less than symbol.
- Review with your child the greater than/less than symbol.
  - > <
  - The big ends points to the big number; the little end points to the little number.
- Day 66 worksheet
- Day 66+ worksheet, Have your child do the first row.

Day 67

- Students will: practice addition facts, review odd and even.
- Review with your child odd and even.
  - An even number of things can be divided evenly. The even numbers end in 2, 4, 6, 8, and 0.
  - An odd number of things has one left over. The odd numbers end in 1, 3, 5, 7, 9.
- Day 67 worksheet
- Day 66+ worksheet, Have your child do the next row.

Day 68

- Students will: practice addition facts, review ordinal numbers, write ordinal numbers.
- Day 66+ worksheet, Have your child do the next row.
- Day 68 worksheet

Day 69

- Students will: practice addition facts, review patterns.
- Day 69 worksheet, Let your child know that the answer doesn't look exactly like the first picture. It just follows the same pattern, such as light, dark, light, dark.
- Day 66+ worksheet, Have your child do the next row.

Day 70

- Students will: solve addition puzzles and drill with known facts.
- Day 66+ worksheet, Have your child do the last row.
- Day 70 worksheet, Help your child see the scale and tell your child that the scale has to balance. There has to be the same amount on each side. You can use your hands to show that you have five on each hand. One hand could be one plus four and the other two plus three, but they would both equal five and balance the scale because they have the same answer.

Geometry

Day 71 (8 crayons – unless your child really doesn't like to color)

- Students will: identify/learn shapes, practice addition facts.
- Day 71 worksheet, Ask your child to identify each shape and tell them the ones they aren't sure of. Have them draw a line to the picture that matches the shape *most closely*.
- Day 71+ worksheet, Have your child do the first line.

Day 72 (6 crayons – unless your child really doesn't like to color)

- Students will: identify/learn shapes, practice addition facts.
- Day 72 worksheet
  - Ask your child what shapes they recognize and if they know what they are called.
  - Tell your child the names of the shapes. (cylinder, cone, cube, rectangular prism or just 3D rectangle, pyramid, sphere)
  - Have them draw a line to the picture that matches the shape *most closely*.
- Day 71+ worksheet, Have your child do the next line.

Day 73 (crayons, five colors)

- Students will: identify shapes, practice addition facts.
- Day 71+ worksheet, Have your child do the next line.
- Day 73 worksheet, Students need to understand that the two parts go together. Once they color in the top that becomes the key to how they should color the shapes inside the bugs.

Day 74 (scissors, You can cut this from your workbook, make your own, or print the
        Tangram pieces from the site. They are on Day 74 on the Math 1 page on Easy
        Peasy.)

- Students will: combine shapes to make new shapes, practice addition facts.
- Day 71+ worksheet, Have your child do the next line.
- Day 74 worksheet, You'll need to cut out the shapes for your child. Encourage
  them to not only make the suggested pictures.

Day 75

- Students will: identify shapes, practice addition facts.
- Day 71+ worksheet, Have your child do the last line.
- Day 75 worksheet, Use a piece of paper to cover the names of the shapes. See what
  shapes your child can identify on each line. Then let your child color the shapes.

Day 76

- Students will: identify 2D shapes, write shape names, practice addition facts.
- Ask your child to draw a triangle.
  - Ask your child to count how many sides the triangle has.
    - three
  - Ask your child how many wheels a tricycle has.
    - Three
  - Help your child hear the tri- pattern.
- Show your child this picture of a stop sign.
  - And ask your child to count how many sides it has.
    - eight
  - Ask your child how many legs an octopus has?
    - eight
  - Help your child to hear the oct- pattern.

- Show your child the picture of the Pentagon on the following page and ask your
  child to count the sides.

- A pentagon has five sides. A hexagon has six sides.
- Day 76 worksheet
- Day 76+ worksheet, Have your child do the first line.

Day 77

- Students will: identify 3D shapes, practice addition facts.
- Day 76+ worksheet, Have your child do the next line.
- Day 77 worksheet

Day 78

- Students will: draw shapes, write shape names, practice addition facts.
- Day 76+ worksheet, Have your child do the next line.
- Day 78 worksheet

Day 79 (optional: crayons for coloring)

- Students will: identify shapes, count, practice addition facts.
- Day 76+ worksheet, Have your child do the next line.
- Day 79 worksheet, If your child wants, they could color the picture.

Day 80

- Students will: identify shapes, write shape names, practice addition facts.
- Day 76+ worksheet, Have your child do the last line.
- Day 80 worksheet, You can show your child how they can look up how to spell the words on the Day 75 page, if they are asking you how to spell things.

Fractions

Day 81

- Students will be introduced to fractions.
- Read through this lesson with your child.
    - Fractions are part of a whole number. You already know more about fractions than you think.
    - When you break a candy bar in half in order to share it with someone, that's a fraction. You each have one half.
    - We write that as a one over a two with a line in between. (You should write ½ for your child to show them.)
    - Show your child the picture of the small pizza cut into four slices.

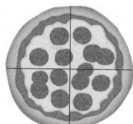

    - If there are four people and four slices, how many pieces can each person have?
        - 1
    - We write, ¼. You can write that 1 over 4 for your child.
    - That fraction means one of the four.
    - That's how you write it in math language. We say "one fourth."
    - Ask your child if the pizza is divided into two parts.
        - No, it's divided into quarters, into four parts.
- For today's worksheet, they will be finding shapes that are divided in half.
    - Ask your child how many pieces are there if something is divided in half.
        - two
    - Make sure your child knows the shape needs to have just two parts and that the two sides have to be equal, just like you are dividing something in half to share.
- Day 81 worksheet

Day 82

- Students will identify representations of fractions with four in the denominator.
- Show your child the square on this page and draw a line down the middle to divide it in half.
    - Ask your child to color in half of the square.
    - Ask your child how many parts are there in the square.
        - 2
    - Ask your child how many of the parts are colored in.
        - 1
    - Write ½ . That shows that one of the two parts is colored in.
- Draw a second line to divide it in half the other way, so that there are four small squares.
    - Ask your child how many parts are there in the square now.
        - 4
    - Ask your child how many of the parts are colored in.
        - 2
    - Write 2/4 for your child with the two over the four. That shows that two of the four parts are colored in.
    - Have your child color in one more of the little squares.
    - Ask how many of the squares are colored in now.
        - 3
    - Ask your child if there are still four parts.
        - Yes
    - Show your child what three fourths looks like, ¾ . That fraction shows three of the four parts are colored in.
- Day 82 worksheet, Tell your child they will be finding the fraction that tells how many of the squares are colored in.

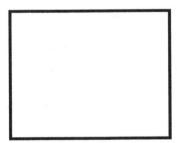

Day 83 (crayons)

- Students will: drill addition facts, color in fractional parts of the whole and design their own flags.
- Day 83 worksheet
- Ask your child about their flag. Ask your child how many parts are on this flag. (3 or 4) How many did you color in blue? (for instance, 1 of the 3 parts, 1/3)
- Quiz your child from the math facts list.

Day 84

- Students will: count, practice addition facts.
- Day 84 worksheet

Day 85

- Students will identify half of a given number of objects and drill addition facts.
- Ask your child to look at these eight dots.
  - Ask your child to figure out how many are half.
- Day 85 worksheet
- Quiz your child from the math facts list.

Day 86 (optional: crayons for coloring)

- Students will: read fractions, make representations of fractions.
- Day 86 worksheet, Go to the page with your child and read the fraction names together.
- Quiz your child from your addition facts list.

Day 87 (optional: crayons for coloring)

- Students will: read fractions, make representations of fractions.
- Day 87 worksheet, Go to the page and read the fraction names together. Teach them how you read 3/8, three eighths.
- Quiz your child from your addition facts list.

Day 88 (optional: crayons for coloring)

- Students will: read fractions, make representations of fractions.
- Day 88 worksheet, Have your child read some of the fractions to you.
- Quiz your child from your addition facts list.

Day 89

- Students will read fraction words and demonstrate understanding of fractions.
- Ask your child how many parts a shape would have if it was in halves. If your child isn't sure, you can explain that one half and one half is two halvesAsk your child how many parts a shape would have if it was in fifths. (5)
- Day 89 worksheet
- Quiz your child from your addition facts list.

Day 90

- Students will practice addition facts and solve for missing numbers in equations.
- Day 90 worksheet

Money

Day 91 (brown crayon, pennies – If you don't have American money, just use the worksheets in the coming days to learn about the coins, and then play with/learn about your own currency. They usually use the same numbers.)

- Students will: learn to identify a penny, learn the value of a penny, find the total amount of money by counting pennies, practice addition facts.
- Get out some pennies and let your child look at them.
   - Each penny is worth one cent or 1₵.
   - Have your child count a handful of pennies.
   - However many there are, that's how many cents you have.
- Day 91 worksheet
- Quiz your child on the addition facts.

Day 92 (nickels)

- Students will: count by fives, be introduced to nickels, find the value of a group of nickels, practice addition facts.
- Count by fives for your child and then ask your child to join you.
- Have your child count by fives.
- Give your child some nickels to look at.
   - Have your child put a handful of nickels in a row.
   - Have your child touch each one and count by fives.
   - That's how many cents you have.
- Day 92 worksheet
- Quiz your child on some addition facts.

Day 93 (dimes)

- Students will: count by tens, be introduced to dimes, find the value of a group of dimes, practice addition facts.
- Have your child count by tens.
- Give your child some dimes to look at.
   - Have your child put a handful of dimes in a row.
   - Have your child touch each one and count by tens.
   - That's how many cents you have.
- Day 93 worksheet
- Quiz your child on some addition facts.

Day 94 (pennies and nickels, brown crayon)

- Students will: find the value of a group of coins, practice addition facts.
- Take out some pennies and nickels. Have your child separate them into a pile of each.
    - Take one nickel and a few pennies.
        - Show your child how to count the nickel first and then count on the pennies.
    - Add another nickel in front and another penny or two.
        - Have your child count the amount of cents by counting the nickels by fives and then counting on the pennies. Help your child along.
    - If your child didn't get it on their own, try another. Add on one more nickel and take off a few pennies.
        - Note: The worksheet will always have the nickels first. It's easiest to start with the largest amount and count on from there.
- Day 94 worksheet

Day 95 (crayon/s)

- Students will: practice addition facts, develop memory skills, count backward, identify even numbers.
- Quiz your child on all the math facts from your facts sheet.
- Play a memory game. Remembering is easiest when you make connections. Instead of letters or numbers, this time let's use our bodies as our connection. "I put a parrot on my head."... "I put a parrot on my head, a cup on my eyebrow, a frog on my nose, a paperclip on my chin, a napkin on my neck, a puzzle on my shoulder, a computer on my arm, etc., elbow, fingers, belly, hip, thigh, knee, calf, heel, toes.

Day 96 (pennies and dimes, brown crayon)

- Students will: find the value of a group of coins, practice addition facts.
- Take out some pennies and dimes. Have your child separate them into a pile of each.
    - Take one dime and a few pennies.
        - Show your child how to count the dime first and then count on the pennies.
    - Add another dime in front and another penny or two.
        - Have your child count the amount of cents by counting the dimes by tens and then counting on the pennies. Help your child along.
    - Add on one more dime and take off a few pennies. Have your child count the amount of money in cents.
        - Note: The worksheet will always have the dimes first. It's easiest to start with the largest amount and count on from there.
- Day 96 worksheet
- Quiz your child from your addition facts sheet.

Day 97 (dimes and nickels)

- Students will: find the value of a group of coins.
- Take out some dimes and nickels. Have your child separate them into piles.
    - Take one nickel and one dime.
        - Show your child how to count the dime first and then count by five to add on the nickel.
    - Add another nickel, and ask your child how much money there is now?
        - 20 cents
    - Add another dime and another nickel.
        - Have your child start with the dimes to count by tens and then count by fives to add on the nickels.
        - Have them touch each one as they count to keep track of where they are.
        - Practice with different amounts until your child is comfortable doing it on their own.
- Day 97 worksheet

Day 98 (quarters)

- Students will: be introduced to quarters, find the value of a group of quarters, practice addition facts.
- Give your child some quarters to look at.
    - Have your child put four quarters in a row.
    - Tell your child how to count quarters.
        - Point to each one and count on: 25, 50, 75, 100.
        - Have your child practice with you until they can do it on their own.
        - Tell your child that 100 cents equals one dollar. If they take 100 cents to the bank, they can exchange it for a one dollar bill.
- Day 98 worksheet
- Quiz your child on addition facts from your sheet.

Day 99 (brown crayon)

- Students will: identify coins, find the amount a group of coins is worth.
- Day 99 worksheet
- Let your child empty your purse or coin cup and get counting.
    - Have them organize the coins into piles and count the amount of cents in each pile.

Day 100

- Students will: practice addition facts, find numbers missing from equations.
- Day 100 worksheet

Day 101 (brown crayon)

- Students will: add the value of nickels and pennies, practice addition facts.
- Day 101 worksheet
- Quiz your child on some addition facts.

Day 102 (brown crayon)

- Students will: practice addition facts, add the value of dimes, nickels and pennies.
- Day 102 worksheet
- Quiz your child on some addition facts.

Day 103 (brown crayon)

- Students will: practice addition facts, add the value of quarters, dimes, nickels and pennies.
- Take a look at the hundreds chart on Day 3. Have your child find twenty-five, what one quarter is worth.
  - Ask your child to figure out what would a quarter and a dime be worth. They need to add ten to 25.
    - They can count this out, but then show them how you can jump down the chart to add ten because when they add ten it's like counting by tens and only the twenty, thirty, forty,...part of the number will change.
  - Ask them to figure out what a quarter and two dimes would be worth.
  - If they need more practice, do it with three and four dimes as well.
- Day 103 worksheet
- Quiz your child on some addition facts.

Day 104 (brown crayon)

- Students will: use greater than/less than and equal signs, add the value of quarters, dimes, nickels and pennies.
- Remind your child about < > =.
  - The big ends points to the big number.
  - The little ends points to the little number. If the numbers are the same, they are equal.
- Day 104 worksheet

Day 105 (crayon/s)

- Students will: practice addition facts, review even numbers, develop memory.
- Make sure your child remembers what numbers are even.
  - They are the numbers that end in 0, 2, 4, 6, and 8.
  - (Continued on the next page...)

- Day 105 worksheet
- Play a memory game. "I went to the park and saw a puppy that was amazing." Keep going adding on adjectives, words that describe the puppy.

Graphs

Day 106 (some of each of four types of coins, vary the number of each, Legos or blocks)

- Students will: practice addition facts, be introduced to bar graphs, build their own 3D bar graph.
- Get out a handful of coins.
- Separate them into groups: all pennies into one group, all quarters into one group (or whatever currency you are using).
- Day 106 worksheet.
  - Draw your coins in their columns. If you have four nickels, draw four circles in the nickel column.
  - Now count up how many are in each group and write it down. For example, if you have 5 pennies, write 5 in the pennies box.
- Now get Legos or some kind of block.
  - Make a tower for each type of coin.
  - Get red Legos and if you have 4 pennies, then build a tower with 4 red Legos.
  - Do that for each coin. Use a different colored Lego for each tower.
    - Here's another example. If you have 6 nickels, then take 6 blue Legos and build a tower.
- When you have all of your towers, line them up next to each other. This is a bar graph.
- Day 106+ worksheet, Have your child do the first line.

Day 107 (handful of coins, fewer than 8 of each type of coin, 4 crayons)

- Students will: draw a bar graph to represent gathered data, practice addition facts.
- Separate the coins into groups and then have your child count them.
  - Their bar graph will only have space for 8 of one type of coin. The graph will look better if the amounts of each type of coin are different.
- Day 107 worksheet
  - Have your child count the number of each type of coin and write that number in the boxes at the top of the page.
  - Then they will draw a bar graph. Instead of building blocks, they will color in the number of blocks. If they have 4 pennies, then they will color in four blocks in the penny column.
  - They are instructed to use a different color for each coin. It's not necessary, but it makes each column stand out.
- Day 106+ worksheet, Have your child do the next line.

Day 108 (4 crayons, up to ten of four different things – spoons, pencils, toy cars, etc…)

- Students will: create a bar graph, practice addition facts.
- Ask your child to gather up some of four different things.
    - You could do coins again, but maybe you want to do spoons or pencils or toy cars or zebras.
    - There's space on the graph for up to ten of each, but they should all be a different amount.
- Day 108 worksheet
    - Your child will do the same thing. You might want to help label their graph and write at the bottom of each column what it represents, such as cars or pencils. You can also give the graph a title.
    - Your child will count the amount of each item and color in that many blocks in that column. (It's fine to just color in things like this with just a pencil.)
- Day 106+ worksheet, Have your child do the next line.

Day 109 (5 crayons)

- Students will: create a bar graph from given data, practice addition facts.
- Day 109 worksheet
    - Your child will count each fruit and write in that number on the given line.
    - Then, like before, your child will use a different color for each fruit and color in the matching number of blocks in the column to show how many of that type of fruit there is.
- Day 106+ worksheet, Have your child do the next line.

Day 110

- Students will: practice addition facts, build memory skills.
- Day 106+ worksheet, Have your child do the last line.
- Day 110 worksheet, Your child will solve the puzzle by solving the addition equations.
- Play a memory game. Play memory music. Make a sound and then build your song by each person adding on a sound and including the sound that came before.

Day 111 (green, red, yellow crayons)

- Students will: create a pie chart to represent given data, practice addition facts.
- Tell your child that they are going to make a new kind of graph today. It's called a pie graph or a pie chart. Like a bar graph it shows how many there are of each thing with a picture of colors.
- Day 111 worksheet
    - Have your child count the number of bees.
        - 3
    - Have your child color in three slices of the pie with yellow.

- o   Ask your child to do the same thing with the other bugs.
- Have your child look at the chart and see which color has the most. A graph lets us quickly see the differences in amounts.
- Day 111+ worksheet, Have your child do the first line.

Day 112 (red, blue, green, yellow crayons)

- Students will: create a pie chart to represent given data, practice addition facts.
- Day 112 worksheet
  - o   Your child will count the number there are of each coin and write it down.
  - o   They will use those numbers to color in the chart. There is a key on the right saying which color to use to represent each coin.
- Day 111+ worksheet, Have your child do the next line.

Day 113

- Students will: read and understand a pictograph, practice addition facts.
- Day 113 worksheet
  - o   Show your child the pictograph and read the title and first sentence.
  - o   Ask your child what the words along the bottom mean.
    - ▪   They are the types of animals represented by the pictures above.
  - o   Ask your child what they think the numbers up the side mean?
    - ▪   Those are the number of each kind of animal.
  - o   Ask your child how many cats the graph shows that their friends have.
    - ▪   4
  - o   Have your child answer the questions.
- Day 111+ worksheet, Have your child do the next line.

Day 114

- Students will: read and understand a bar graph, practice addition facts.
- Day 114 worksheet
  - o   Show your child the graph and ask them what type of graph it is.
    - ▪   bar graph
  - o   Read the title and first sentence.
  - o   Ask your child what they think the pictures along the bottom mean.
    - ▪   They are the types of animals represented by the columns above them.
  - o   Ask your child what they think the numbers up the side mean?
    - ▪   Those are the number of each kind of animal.
  - o   Ask your child how many birds the graph shows that their friends have.
    - ▪   1
    - ▪   It goes up to the first line. It's pretty easy to see that it's one for the bird. Stay with your child as they answer the first question to make sure they are understanding how to read it. There are 4 cats.
- Day 111+ worksheet, Have your child do the next line.

30

Day 115 (1 or 6 crayons)

- Students will: read a pictograph pie chart, practice addition facts.
- Day 115 worksheet
  - Show your child the pie graph and read the title and directions.
  - The first box is for elephants. Ask your child how many elephants are represented on the graph.
    - 2
    - They should write 2 in the first box.
  - After they finish filling in the numbers, they will color in a bar graph showing how many there are of each animal. Each bar can be the same color.
- Day 111+ worksheet, Have your child do the last line.

Subtraction

Day 116 (five of the same objects: coins, blocks, etc.)

- Students will: understand the concept of subtraction, subtract with objects.
- Do this subtraction comprehension activity with your child.
  - Take your five objects and have your child lay them out and count them.
  - Pick up one of them, and ask your child how many are there now.
    - 4
  - There are four down and one in your hand. Four plus one equals five. Now we are seeing that five take away one is four. In math we say: five minus one equals four.
    - Show your child what the subtraction equation and minus sign looks like, $5 - 1 = 4$.
    - Have them repeat the words subtraction and minus.
- Start a subtraction facts list and write $5 - 1 = 4$
- Let your child play with your five objects. If they take away two, how many are left? What if they take away all five?
- Day 116 worksheet
  - If it's too hard for your child to write the number words on the line, they can read you the number sentence and say it out loud.

Day 117 (ten of the same objects: coins, blocks, etc.)

- Students will: understand the concept of taking away one, subtract with a number line.
- Do this subtraction comprehension activity with your child.
  - Take your ten objects and have your child lay five out and count them.
    - Add on one block. $5 + 1 = 6$ Say it out loud, "Five plus one equals six."

- Add another block. $6 + 1 = 7$ Each time say the math problem out loud.
        - Add another block. $7 + 1 = 8$
        - Add another block. $8 + 1 = 9$
        - Add another block. $9 + 1 = 10$
    - Now take away a block. $10 - 1 = 9$ Say it out loud, "Ten minus one equals nine."
    - Take away another block. $9 - 1 = 8$ Continue to say each problem out loud.
    - Continue until you have no blocks.
- Day 117 worksheet
    - Show your child the number line. Have your child start at ten and jump to each number and say the subtraction sentence. "Ten minus one is nine. Nine minus one is eight...."
    - Have your child complete the worksheet.

Day 118

- Students will: understand the concept of subtracting zero and all, practice subtracting with zero, one, and all.
- Ask your child these subtraction comprehension questions.
    - If you had 100 blocks, and I took all 100 away, how many blocks would you have? (answer: zero)
    - If you had 1 million blocks, and I took away 1 million blocks, how many blocks would you have? (answer: zero)
    - If you had one block, and you gave me one block, how many blocks would you have? (answer: zero)
    - If you had five blocks, and you didn't give me any, how many blocks would you have? (answer: you would still have five blocks)
    - If you had nine blocks, and you gave me zero blocks, how many blocks would you have? (answer: nine)
    - If you have seven blocks, and I took from you zero blocks, how many blocks would you have? (answer: seven)
- Day 118 worksheet

Day 119

- Students will: practice addition facts, practice subtracting with zero, one, and all.
- Day 119 worksheet
- Quiz your child on some addition facts.

Day 120

- Students will: practice subtracting with objects, practice addition facts.
- Day 120 worksheet
- Quiz your child on some addition facts.

Subtraction Introduction continued and Fraction Review

Day 121

- Students will: be introduced to fact families, use what they know to fill in missing math symbols.
- Review subtraction with your child.
    - When we subtract, we take away from what we already have.
    - If you have 5 and take 0 away, you still have 5.
    - If you have 5 and take 1 away, you have four.
    - That's 5 minus 1 equals 4. $5 - 1 = 4$ (Show the equation to your child or have them write it.)
- Introduce fact families.
    - Subtraction is the opposite of addition. If you have four and add back on one, then you have five. (You can use your fingers to show it.)
    - These facts are all relatives because they use the same numbers. We call them a fact family. (You can use your fingers to show these problems.)
        - $1 + 4 = 5$
        - $4 + 1 = 5$
        - $5 - 1 = 4$
        - $5 - 4 = 1$
- Introduce subtraction when the answer is one.
    - Turn to Day 117 in the workbook.
    - Have your child point to a number on the number line. Ask your child what numbers are next to it.
    - Whenever you see a subtraction problem with the two numbers right next to each other on the number line (like 5 and 4 or 6 and 7 or 8 and 9) then the answer will be one.
    - If you have nine candies and I take eight, then you will only have one left.
    - Use the number your child pointed to. If they had that many toys, and you took away (the number right before it), how many would they have left?
- Day 121 worksheet, Your child will be filling in a minus sign or a plus sign.

Day 122

- Students will: identify fractions represented by pictures, practice subtraction with 0 and 1 in the problem and as the difference.
- Ask your child to draw five circles.
    - Write the fraction 2/5 with the two over the five.
    - Ask your child to color in some of the circles so that two fifths of them are colored.
    - The bottom number, the denominator, shows how many parts. In this case, it shows how many circles.
    - The top number, the numerator, shows how many are colored in.
    - Note: They don't need to know and use these words, but it doesn't hurt to introduce them.

- Ask your child how many pencils would be left if you had five and then took five away.
  - You would have nothing left, zero.
- Ask your child how many would be left if you only took away four of the five pencils.
  - You would still have one left.
- Day 122 worksheet

Day 123

- Students will: count to subtract, learn the subtraction fact 5 – 3 = 2.
- Have your child demonstrate 5 – 3 = 2 and 5 – 2 = 3 with their fingers or toys or whatever.
- Write those new facts on the subtraction facts list. Write both down.
- Have your child look at the facts and read them out loud.
- Day 123 worksheet, Have your child cross out the number being subtracted and then count up how many remain.
- Quiz your child on the subtraction fact from today and the addition facts.

Day 124 (crayon/s)

- Students will: represent fractions with pictures, practice subtraction facts.
- Day 124 worksheet, They will color in the number of spaces shown by the top number.
- When you check their page, have them read the fractions to you.

Day 125 (crayon/s)

- Students will: represent fractions with pictures, practice addition and subtraction facts.
- Day 124 worksheet, They will color in the number of spaces shown by the top number.
- Quiz your child using the addition facts sheet.

Subtraction

Day 126 (five coins, or anything for subtraction practice)

- Students will: identify the relationship between addition and subtraction facts, practice with fact families 1/4/5 and 2/3/5.
- Do this fact family comprehension activity.
  - Have your child lay out the five coins or whatever you are using.

- o Move one coin over to the side. Tell your child that it shows two addition problems. Do they know what they are? If not, give the first one, 1 plus 4 equals 5.
  - $1 + 4 = 5$
  - $4 + 1 = 5$
- o Tell your child it also shows two subtraction problems. Do they know what they are?
  - $5 - 1 = 4$
  - $5 - 4 = 1$
- o Now move another coin so that there are two in the one pile and three in the other. See if your child can identify two addition and two subtraction problems.
  - $2 + 3 = 5$
  - $3 + 2 = 5$
  - $5 - 3 = 2$
  - $5 - 2 = 3$
- o These are fact families. The addition and subtraction problems use the same numbers. They are just the opposites of each other. One takes away and one puts back.
- o Day 126 worksheet

Day 127 (six coins or something to use for subtracting objects)

- Students will: learn the 3/3/6 and 2/2/4 fact families, practice known facts.
- Get out blocks or coins or something and show that $3 + 3 = 6$ and $6 - 3 = 3$ as well as $2 + 2 = 4$ and $4 - 2 = 2$.
- Add these to your subtraction facts list.(Check them off and if you are making cards or another kind of list, begin adding each new fact as it's learned.)
- Day 127 worksheet
- Quiz your child from your addition facts list.

Day 128 (six coins or something to use for subtracting objects)

- Students will: learn the 2/4/6 fact family, practice known facts.
- Get out blocks or coins or something and show that $2 + 4 = 6$ and $6 - 4 = 2$ as well as $4 + 2 = 6$ and $6 - 2 = 4$.
- Add these to your subtraction facts list.
- Day 128 worksheet

Day 129

- Students will: learn the 4/4/8 fact family, practice known facts.
- Hold up four fingers on each hand and practice the 4/4/8 fact family.
  - $4 + 4 = 8$
  - $8 - 4 = 4$
- Add this to your subtraction facts list.
- Day 129 worksheet

Day 130

- Students will: learn the 5/5/10 fact family, develop memory muscle.
- Hold up five fingers on each hand and practice the 5/5/10 fact family.
  - $5 + 5 = 10$
  - $10 - 5 = 5$
- Add this to your subtraction facts list.
- Day 130 worksheet
- Play the memory game. "Today I saw an apricot." "Today I saw an apricot and a baboon." Etc…

Day 131

- Students will: practice with known addition and subtraction facts.
- Day 131 worksheet
- Quiz your child from your addition facts sheet.

Day 132

- Students will: learn the 3/4/7 fact family, practice known facts.
- Ask your child $3 + 4$ and $4 + 3$.
  - 7
- Ask your child what $7 - 4$ would be?
  - If they aren't sure, ask four plus what equals seven.
  - Four plus three equals seven, so seven minus four equals three.
- Ask your child what $7 - 3$ would be?
  - 4
- Add these to your subtraction facts list.
- Day 132 worksheet

Day 133

- Students will: learn the 2/5/7 fact family, practice known facts.
- Ask your child $2 + 5$ and $5 + 2$.
  - 7
- (Continued on the next page…)

- Ask your child what 7 – 5 would be?
  - If they aren't sure, ask five plus what equals seven.
  - Five plus two equals seven, so seven minus five equals two.
- Ask your child what 7 – 5 would be?
  - 2
- Add these to your subtraction facts list.
- Day 133 worksheet
- Quiz your child on addition facts from your list.

Day 134

- Students will: learn the 3/5/8 fact family, practice known facts.
- Ask your child 3 + 5 and 5 + 3.
  - 8
- Ask your child what 8 – 5 would be?
  - If they aren't sure, ask five plus what equals eight.
  - Five plus three equals eight, so eight minus five equals three.
- Ask your child what 8 – 3 would be?
  - 5
- Add these to your subtraction facts list.
- Day 134 worksheet

Day 135

- Students will: practice special fact families, practice known facts.
- Day 135 worksheet
- Quiz your child from your facts lists.

Day 136

- Students will: count down to subtract, practice addition facts.
- Day 136 worksheet

Day 137

- Students will: learn the 4/5/9 fact family, practice known facts.
- Hold up both hands with just four fingers up on one hand.
- Ask your child how many fingers are up on each hand and all together.
- Ask your child what addition problem that shows.
  - $4 + 5 = 9$
  - $5 + 4 = 9$
- (Continued on the next page…)

- Ask your child what 9 – 5 would be?
  - If they aren't sure, show your hands and take away the one with five fingers up.
  - Five plus four equals nine, so nine minus five equals four.
- Ask your child what 9 – 4 would be?
  - 5
- Add these to your subtraction facts list.
- Day 137 worksheet

Day 138

- Students will: practice known addition and subtraction facts.
- Day 138 worksheet
- Quiz your child on facts from your addition facts list.

Day 139

- Students will: practice known subtraction facts.
- Day 139 worksheet

Day 140 (optional: crayons for coloring)

- Students will: practice known subtraction facts, build memory skills.
- Day 140 worksheet
- Play the memory game. "On our trip across the country I saw one goat." "On our trip across the country I saw one goat and two billboards." Etc… Use numbers as your memory hook.

Review Money

Day 141 (brown crayon)

- Students will: practice known addition facts, review identifying nickels and pennies, adding coin values.
- Day 141+ worksheet, Have your child do the first line. Make sure they pay attention to whether it is addition or subtraction.
- Day 141 worksheet

Day 142 (brown crayon)

- Students will: practice known subtraction facts, review identifying nickels and pennies, adding coin values.
- Day 141+ worksheet, Have your child do the next line. Make sure they pay attention to whether it is addition or subtraction.

- Day 142 worksheet, They should always start with the highest amount and then count on from there.

Day 143

- Students will: practice known addition facts, counting the value of dimes.
- Ask your child how much a dime is worth and how they would find how much three dimes was worth.
  - ten cents, count by tens
- Day 141+ worksheet, Have your child do the next line. Make sure they pay attention to whether it is addition or subtraction.
- Day 143 worksheet

Day 144 (optional: crayons for coloring)

- Students will: practice known subtraction facts, counting the value of quarters.
- Day 141+ worksheet, Have your child do the next line.
- Day 144 worksheet

Day 145 (brown crayon)

- Students will: practice known addition facts, identify coins, add coin values, compare money amounts.
- Day 141+ worksheet, Have your child do the last line.
- Day 145 worksheet

Review graphs, fractions

Day 146 (5 crayons)

- Students will: create a bar graph from given data, practice known subtraction facts.
- Day 146+ worksheet, Have your child do the first line. Make sure they pay attention each day to whether it is addition or subtraction.
- Day 146 worksheet
  - This is a review of bar graphs.
  - They will count the number of each shape. They could put a mark or color each one to show it's been counted.
  - They will write the number of each shape and then color in that many blocks in the graph below.

Day 147

- Students will: read a pie graph, practice known addition facts, add multiple addends.
- Day 146+ worksheet, Have your child do the next line. Make sure they pay attention each day to whether it is addition or subtraction.
- Day 147 worksheet
  - This is a review of pie graphs.
  - They will count the number of each shape.
  - They will write the number of each shape and then find the total number of shapes.
  - They will use those numbers in the second part of the page.

Day 148 (crayons)

- Students will: create visual representations of fractions, practice known subtraction facts.
- Day 146+ worksheet, Have your child do the next line. Make sure they pay attention each day to whether it is addition or subtraction.
- Day 148 worksheet
  - This is a review of fractions.
  - Make sure your child knows that the denominator, the bottom number, shows the number of parts and that the numerator, the top number, shows the number they should color in.
  - Ask your child to read the first fraction to you. It's ½, one half.
  - Can your child read some of the others? It's okay if you need to help.

Day 149 (crayon/s)

- Students will: identify fractions from visual representations, practice known addition facts.
- Day 146+ worksheet, Have your child do the next line. Make sure they pay attention each day to whether it is addition or subtraction.
  - Day 149 worksheet, This is a review of fractions.
  - They will count the number of pieces and the number colored in and match that to the choices.
  - At the bottom they have to color in the correct number of pieces from reading the fraction words.

Day 150

- Students will: practice known subtraction facts.
- Day 146+ worksheet, Have your child do the last line.
- Day 150 worksheet, If they are correct, the last box will be the answer from both directions.

Time

Day 151 (optional: crayons for coloring)

- Students will: practice known addition facts, learn to read a clock on the hour.
- Day 151+ worksheet, Have your child do the first line.
- Day 151 worksheet
  - Tell your child that the lines on a clock are called hands.
  - Show your child how every clock on the page has a hand pointing to the twelve.
    - That's the long hand, and it tells us how many minutes after the hour it is.
    - When it's pointing straight up, it's zero minutes after the hour. It's when we say it's "o'clock."
  - Show your child how there is a shorter hand as well. That's the hour hand. It's shorter because we don't have to know precisely where it is.
    - Ask your child what number the short hand is pointing to on the first clock.
      - 3
    - Show and tell your child that the hour hand doesn't stay still. It will keep moving slowly the whole hour until it is pointing to the four. So when it's pointing anywhere between 3 and 4, the hour is still three.
  - Tell your child that since the hour hand is pointing to three and the minute hand is pointing to twelve, the clock says that it's three o'clock.
  - Show your child the answer. That's what three o'clock looks like on a digital clock.
  - Let your child try the rest.

Day 152 (optional: crayons for coloring)

- Students will: practice subtraction facts, read analog clocks and write digital times on the hour.
- Day 151+ worksheet, Have your child do the next line.
- Day 152 worksheet, Review with your child the minute and hour hands. This time they have to write the digital time, like how it shows on a computer. If they are unsure, they can look at the page before.
- From the Math 1 page on our site, you can print out a clock with hands to cut out that you can put together and practice time with. Find it on Day 152.

Day 153 (optional: crayons for coloring)

- Students will: practice addition and subtraction facts, draw hands on analog clocks from their digital or written time.
- Day 151+ worksheet, Have your child do the next line.
- Day 153 worksheet, Review with your child the minute and hour hands. This time they have to draw the hands. Tell them that all of the times are "o'clock" times. Where will the long minute hand point on each clock?
  - straight up to the twelve
- Quiz your child from your subtraction facts list.

Day 154

- Students will: practice subtraction facts, draw hands on analog clocks, find the new time after time elapses.
- Day 151+ worksheet, Have your child do the next line.
- Day 154 worksheet, Have your child draw the hands on the first clock, 1:00. Show your child that they can use the clock like a number line. They can count on three hours to get to four o'clock. They will write 4:00 and draw the hands on the second clock.

Day 155 (optional: crayons for coloring)

- Students will: practice addition and subtraction facts, read analog clocks and write digital times on the half hour.
- Day 151+ worksheet, Have your child do the last line.
- Day 155 worksheet
  - Review with your child the minute and hour hands.
  - Ask your child what number the minute hand is pointing to on every clock.
  - This time it is pointing to the six.
  - Show your child the clock on the next page and point out the small lines that show the minutes.
    - Have your child start counting the lines. The twelve marks 0 in our counting, so the first line after the twelve is one.
    - (This lesson continues on the next page.)

- o Show your child how each big number is five more and that they can count by fives to count minutes quickly. Point to each big number and count by fives.
- o Ask your child to count by fives until they get to the six. They should touch the one and say, "Five," and count from there. They should say, "Thirty," when they get to the six.
  - ▪ When the minute hand is pointing to the six, it's thirty minutes after the hour.
- o Have your child look at the first clock on the worksheet. What time do they think it is?
  - ▪ Remind them that the hour hand is always moving. Since the minute hand is halfway around the clock, the hour hand is halfway between the three and four.
  - ▪ It's three thirty.

Day 156 (optional: crayons for coloring)

- • Students will: practice subtraction facts, tell time to the half hour.
- • Day 156 + worksheet, Have your child do the first line.
- • Day 156 worksheet

Day 157 (optional: crayons for coloring)

- Students will: practice addition and subtraction facts, tell time to the half hour.
- Day 156 + worksheet, Have your child do the next line.
- Day 157 worksheet
- Quiz your child on subtraction facts from your facts list.

Day 158

- Students will: practice addition and subtraction facts, tell time to the half hour, figure out the new time after time elapses, draw hands on clocks.
- Day 156 + worksheet, Have your child do the next line.
- Day 158 worksheet, Have your child draw the hands on the first clock. Remind your child how they can use the clock like a timeline and count on the hours to find the new time.
- Quiz your child on addition facts from your facts list.

Day 159 (optional: crayons for coloring)

- Students will: practice addition and subtraction facts, draw hands on clocks to the hour and half hour, learn the time words "half past."
- Day 156 + worksheet, Have your child do the next line.
- Day 159 worksheet, Ask your child what time it is when the minute hand goes half way around the clock and is pointing to the six.
    - That's thirty minutes, like 1:30. Since it's halfway around the clock and halfway to the next hour, we call that half past. When it's half past one, it's 1:30.
    - What time would it be if it were half past three?
        - 3:30
    - Keep asking your child different hours until it's easy for them.
- Quiz your child on subtraction facts from your facts list.

Day 160 (optional: crayons for coloring)

- Students will: practice addition and subtraction facts, draw hands on clocks to the hour and half hour.
- Day 156 + worksheet, Have your child do the last line.
- Day 160 worksheet
- Quiz your child on addition facts from your facts list.

Patterns/Beginner Algebraic Concepts

Day 161 (optional: crayons for coloring)

- Students will: identify and complete a pattern, tell time on analog and digital clocks.
- Day 161+ worksheet, Have your child do the first line.
- Day 161 worksheet, Sometimes your child will be drawing the hands on the clock. Sometimes they will be writing the digital time. Make sure your child is comfortable with the assignment before they try on their own.

Day 162 (optional: crayons for coloring)

- Students will: identify and complete a pattern, tell time on analog and digital clocks, practice subtraction facts.
- Day 161+ worksheet, Have your child do the next line.
- Day 162 worksheet
- Quiz your child from your subtraction facts list.

Day 163 (optional: crayons for coloring)

- Students will: identify and complete a pattern, tell time on analog and digital clocks.
- Day 161+ worksheet, Have your child do the next line.
- Day 163 worksheet

Day 164 (optional: crayons for coloring)

- Students will: use greater than, less than, and equals symbols, practice known addition and subtraction facts, identify and complete a pattern.
- Day 161+ worksheet, Have your child do the next line.
- Day 164 worksheet
- Quiz your child from your subtraction facts list.

Day 165 (optional: crayons for coloring)

- Students will: use problem solving skills to fill in missing plus and minus signs, practice known addition and subtraction facts, identify and complete a pattern.
- Day 161+ worksheet, Have your child do the last line.
- Day 165 worksheet
- Quiz your child from your addition facts list.

Review

Day 166

- Students will: practice known subtraction facts, demonstrate knowledge of digital and analog time.
- Day 166 worksheet

Day 167

- Students will: practice known subtraction facts, read time words and draw the matching times on analog clock.
- Day 167 worksheet

Day 168

- Students will: practice known subtraction facts, demonstrate knowledge of coin values in combination.
- Day 168 worksheet, Before your child begins, make sure they can recognize each type of coin and how much it is worth.

Day 169

- Students will: practice known subtraction facts, demonstrate knowledge of coin values in combination.
- Day 169 worksheet

Day 170

- Students will: demonstrate ability in addition and subtraction.
- Day 170 worksheet, They are to use their answers from the top part to complete the maze on the bottom of the page.
- Quiz your child from your addition facts list.

Day 171 (brown crayon)

- Students will: practice known subtraction facts, demonstrate knowledge of coin values in combination.
- Day 171 worksheet
- Quiz your child on subtraction facts from your list.

Day 172 (crayon/s)

- Students will: practice known addition facts, demonstrate knowledge of fractions.
- Day 172 worksheet
- Quiz your child on addition facts.

Day 173

- Students will: order numbers.
- Day 173 worksheet

Day 174 (crayon/s)

- Students will: practice addition facts, review odd and even.
- Day 174 worksheet, You might want to check their answers. If they are correct, the even answers (end in 0, 2, 4, 6 and 8) will take them through a maze to the end.

Day 175 (crayon/s)

- Students will: practice subtraction facts, review odd and even.
- Day 175 worksheet, You might want to check their answers. If they are correct, the odd answers (end in 1, 3, 5, 7 and 9) will take them through a maze to the end.

Day 176 (crayon/s)

- Students will: order numbers, demonstrate understanding of odd and even, demonstrate knowledge of addition facts learned this year.
- Day 176 worksheet
- Quiz your child on addition facts from your sheet.

Day 177

- Students will: demonstrate knowledge of addition facts learned this year.
- Day 177 worksheet
- Quiz your child on subtraction facts from your sheet.

Day 178

- Students will: add and subtract to complete fact families.
- Day 178 worksheet

Day 179

- Students will: complete puzzles using addition and subtraction.
- Day 179 worksheet, Make sure your child pays attention to the plus and minus signs.

Day 180

- Students will: complete puzzles using addition and subtraction.
- Day 180 worksheet, Make sure your child pays attention to the plus and minus signs.
- Celebrate your child completing first grade math!

EP Math 1

Workbook Answers

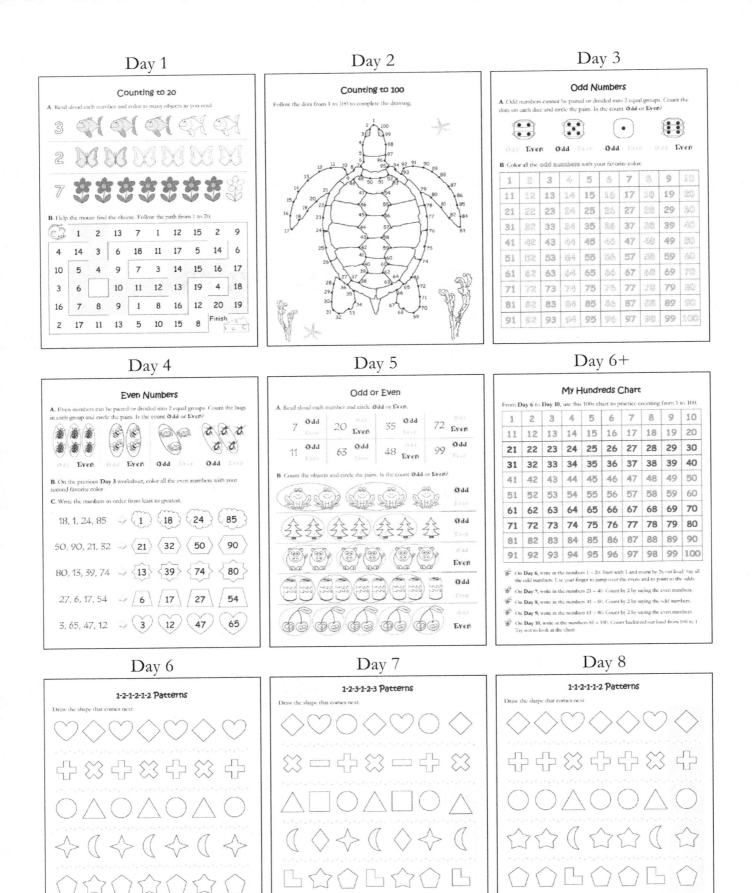

Day 9

Counting by 2s

Count by 2s out loud and fill in the missing numbers.

1	3	5	7	9	11	13

20	22	24	26	28	30	32

35	37	39	41	43	45	47

60	62	64	66	68	70	72

Day 10

Counting by 2s

A. Count by 2s out loud and fill in the missing odd numbers.

5	7	19	21	23	35	37

9	17	25	33

11	13	15	27	29	31

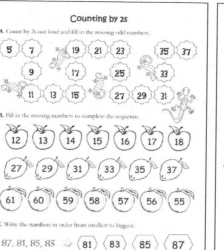

B. Fill in the missing numbers to complete the sequence.

12	13	14	15	16	17	18

27	29	31	33	35	37

61	60	59	58	57	56	55

C. Write the numbers in order from smallest to biggest.

87, 81, 85, 83 → 81 83 85 87

Day 11

Number Words to 10

A. Write your age as a number and a number word.

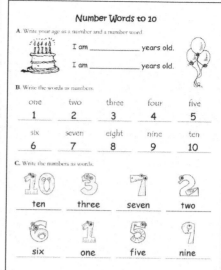

I am _____ years old.

I am _____ years old.

B. Write the words as numbers.

one	two	three	four	five
1	2	3	4	5

six	seven	eight	nine	ten
6	7	8	9	10

C. Write the numbers as words.

ten	three	seven	two

six	one	five	nine

Day 12

Ordinal Numbers to 10

A. Fill in the blanks with ordinal number words.

A is the __first__ letter of the alphabet.

F is the __sixth__ letter of the alphabet.

B. Write the words as numbers.

first	second	third	fourth	fifth
1	2	3	4	5

sixth	seventh	eighth	ninth	tenth
6	7	8	9	10

C. Fill in the blanks with ordinal number words.

third	ninth	first	fourth

eighth	tenth	second	sixth

Day 13

Number Words to 20

A. Write the words as numbers.

eleven	twelve	thirteen	fourteen	fifteen
11	12	13	14	15

sixteen	seventeen	eighteen	nineteen	twenty
16	17	18	19	20

B. Write the numbers as words.

11	eleven	16	sixteen
12	twelve	17	seventeen
13	thirteen	18	eighteen
14	fourteen	19	nineteen
15	fifteen	20	twenty

C. Draw a picture of 7 objects in a line. Circle the first. Draw a line under the third. Draw an X over the fifth. Color the seventh object in the line.

Day 14

Number Words to 30

A. Write the words as numbers.

twenty-one	21	twenty-six	26
twenty-two	22	twenty-seven	27
twenty-three	23	twenty-eight	28
twenty-four	24	twenty-nine	29
twenty-five	25	thirty	30

B. Write the numbers as words.

21	twenty-one
23	twenty-three
24	twenty-four
25	twenty-five
27	twenty-seven
28	twenty-eight
30	thirty

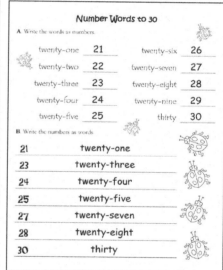

Day 15

Number Words to 100

A. Write the words as numbers.

ten	twenty	thirty	forty	fifty
10	20	30	40	50

sixty	seventy	eighty	ninety	one hundred
60	70	80	90	100

B. Write the numbers as words.

10	ten	60	sixty
20	twenty	70	seventy
30	thirty	80	eighty
40	forty	90	ninety
50	fifty	100	one hundred

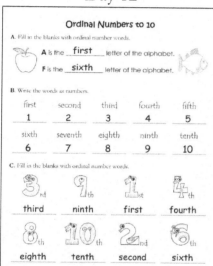

Day 16

Adding 0

A. Put **two** coins in your hand (if you can't find two coins, you can use something else.) Now go and ask your mom (or someone else) to give you **zero more** coins. How many coins do you have in your hand now? Fill in the blanks.

I had __two__ coins and got __zero__ more.

Now I have __two__ coins.

You just learned that 2 plus 0 more is still 2. We say **2 plus 0 equals 2**. We write $2 + 0 = 2$.

B. Put **five** coins in your hand. Go and ask for **zero more** coins. How many coins do you have in your hand now? Fill in the blanks.

I had __five__ coins and got __zero__ more.

Now I have __five__ coins.

We say:	We write:
__5__ plus __0__ equals __5__	__5__ + __0__ = __5__

C. Let's practice adding 0. Use your coins to find the answers.

$4 + 0 = 4$ $0 + 4 = 4$

$7 + 0 = 7$ $0 + 7 = 7$

$1 + 0 = 1$ $0 + 1 = 1$

Day 17

Adding 1

A. Get ten blocks (or coins). Count out **three** blocks and stack them together. Add **one more** block. How many blocks are in your stack now? Fill in the blanks.

I had __three__ blocks and got __one__ more.

Now I have __four__ blocks.

You just learned that 3 plus 1 more is 4. We say **3 plus 1 equals 4**. We write $3 + 1 = 4$.

B. Count out **four** blocks and stack them together. Add **one more** block. How many blocks are in your stack now? Fill in the blanks.

I had __four__ blocks and got __one__ more.

Now I have __five__ blocks.

We say:	We write:
__4__ plus __1__ equals __5__	__4__ + __1__ = __5__

C. Let's practice adding 1. Use your blocks to find the answers.

$5 + 1 = 6$ $1 + 5 = 6$

$8 + 1 = 9$ $1 + 8 = 9$

$6 + 1 = 7$ $1 + 6 = 7$

Day 18

Adding 1 & Ordering Numbers

A. Let's practice adding 1.

6	3	1	8	1	4	7	1
$+1$	$+1$	$+5$	$+1$	$+7$	$+1$	$+1$	$+9$
7	4	6	9	8	5	8	10

	2	5	1	1	9	1
	$+1$	$+1$	$+4$	$+0$	$+1$	$+1$
	3	6	5	1	10	2

B. Write the numbers in order from smallest to biggest.

12, 19, 15, 14 → (12)(14)(15)(19)
46, 48, 41, 40 → (40)(41)(46)(48)
20, 23, 29, 26 → (20)(23)(26)(29)
97, 95, 98, 93 → (93)(95)(97)(98)
69, 68, 62, 64 → (62)(64)(68)(69)

Day 19

Adding 1 on a Number Line

Below is a number line. It can help you add. Put your finger on 0. Jump one number to the right. That adds one. What number are you on now? Write the answer. Jump one more and write that answer. Keep doing the same until you get to ten.

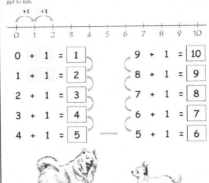

$0 + 1 = 1$		$9 + 1 = 10$
$1 + 1 = 2$		$8 + 1 = 9$
$2 + 1 = 3$		$7 + 1 = 8$
$3 + 1 = 4$		$6 + 1 = 7$
$4 + 1 = 5$		$5 + 1 = 6$

Day 20

Adding 0 and 1 & Ordering Numbers

A. Let's practice adding 0 and 1.

3	1	5	9	0	0	1	0
$+0$	$+6$	$+0$	$+1$	$+2$	$+1$	$+7$	$+6$
3	7	5	10	2	1	8	6

	5	1	1	0	8	1
	$+1$	$+3$	$+1$	$+9$	$+1$	$+4$
	6	4	2	9	9	5

B. Write the numbers in order from biggest to smallest.

36, 39, 35, 38 → (39)(38)(36)(35)
53, 57, 50, 51 → (57)(53)(51)(50)
85, 82, 89, 88 → (89)(88)(85)(82)
73, 79, 77, 74 → (79)(77)(74)(73)
20, 25, 22, 26 → (26)(25)(22)(20)

Day 21

Adding on Number Lines

Below is a number line. It can help you add. Put your finger on 2. Jump three numbers to the right. That adds three. What number are you on now? Right! It's 5. 2 and 3 more is 5. **2 + 3 = 5.**

$2 + 3 = 5$

Use the number line to add. Write the answer in the box.

$3 + 4 = 7$
$2 + 7 = 9$
$0 + 8 = 8$
$1 + 9 = 10$
$3 + 7 = 10$
$4 + 4 = 8$
$2 + 6 = 8$
$1 + 8 = 9$

Day 22

Counting to Add

Count the objects to add. Write the answer in the box.

 = 3

 = 5

= 5

 = 4

= 6

= 10

Day 23

Counting to Add

A. Count the objects to add. Solve each problem and read it out loud.

2		2		3
$+2$		$+3$		$+2$
4 (Two plus two equals four.)		5		5

3		2		4
$+3$		$+4$		$+2$
6		6		6

3		4		4
$+4$		$+3$		$+4$
7		7		8

B. Let's practice adding 0 and 1. Read out loud each problem.

3	1	5	1	0	0	1	0
$+0$	$+6$	$+1$	$+8$	$+2$	$+1$	$+7$	$+9$
3	7	6	9	2	1	8	9

Day 24

Adding Sums up to 4

A. Practice addition up to 2 + 2.

2	0	2	1	2
$+2$	$+2$	$+1$	$+0$	$+0$
4	2	3	1	2

1	1	2	0	2
$+1$	$+2$	$+2$	$+1$	$+1$
2	3	4	1	3

0	1	2	2	1
$+0$	$+1$	$+0$	$+2$	$+2$
0	2	2	4	3

B. Color the owls whose addition sentence equals 4.

1 + 3   4 + 1   2 + 2   4 + 0   2 + 1

Day 25

Adding Sums up to 5

A. Practice addition up to 2 + 3 and 3 + 2.

2	1	2	0	0	3	1	0
$+3$	$+3$	$+2$	$+1$	$+3$	$+2$	$+2$	$+2$
5	4	4	1	3	5	3	2

3	2	3	2	2	1	3	2
$+2$	$+1$	$+1$	$+0$	$+2$	$+1$	$+0$	$+3$
5	3	4	2	4	2	3	5

B. Complete each addition sentence to make 5.

$5 + 0 = 5$
$4 + 1 = 5$
$3 + 2 = 5$
$2 + 3 = 5$
$1 + 4 = 5$
$0 + 5 = 5$

Day 26

Adding Sums up to 6

Practice addition up to 3 + 3.

3	2	3	3	1	3	3	2
$+3$	$+3$	$+2$	$+2$	$+3$	$+3$	$+2$	$+3$
6	5	4	5	4	6	5	5

2	2	1	3	2	3	1	3
$+3$	$+2$	$+1$	$+3$	$+2$	$+3$	$+1$	$+3$
5	4	2	6	5	6	4	6

$3 + 3 = 6$ $3 + 2 = 5$
$0 + 0 = 0$ $1 + 3 = 4$
$3 + 2 = 5$ $2 + 3 = 5$
               $2 + 2 = 4$
               $3 + 1 = 4$
               $3 + 3 = 6$

Day 27

Adding Sums up to 6

A. Practice addition up to 2 + 4 and 4 + 2.

2 +4 = 6	1 +1 = 2	2 +3 = 5	4 +0 = 4	1 +4 = 5	2 +2 = 4	4 +2 = 6	3 +2 = 5
4 +2 = 6	3 +2 = 5	0 +4 = 4	4 +1 = 5	2 +2 = 4	2 +4 = 6	3 +1 = 4	2 +3 = 5

B. Color the animals whose addition sentence equals 6.

1 + 5   2 + 2   3 + 3   2 + 4

2 + 3   4 + 2   3 + 2   0 + 6

Day 28

Adding Sums up to 7

A. Practice addition up to 3 + 4 and 4 + 3.

3 +4 = 7	3 +3 = 6	4 +2 = 6	2 +3 = 5	2 +4 = 6	3 +2 = 5	3 +4 = 7	4 +3 = 7
4 +3 = 7	3 +2 = 5	3 +4 = 7	2 +2 = 4	2 +3 = 5	3 +4 = 7	3 +3 = 6	3 +4 = 7

B. Practice adding sums up to 7.

1 + 6 = 7
2 + 4 = 6
3 + 2 = 5
3 + 3 = 6
7 + 0 = 7
4 + 3 = 7

Day 29

Adding Sums up to 8

Practice addition up to 4 + 4.

4 +4 = 8	2 +4 = 6	2 +3 = 5	4 +3 = 7	2 +2 = 4	3 +4 = 7	
3 +4 = 7	4 +2 = 6	4 +4 = 8	3 +2 = 5	4 +3 = 7	3 +3 = 6	4 +4 = 8
4 +2 = 6	4 +4 = 8	2 +3 = 5	3 +4 = 7	4 +4 = 8	3 +3 = 6	2 +4 = ...

B. Practice adding sums up to 8.

3 + 3 = 6   3 + 4 = 7
4 + 3 = 7   2 + 3 = 5
8 + 0 = 8   4 + 2 = 6
3 + 2 = 5   1 + 7 = 8

Day 30

Adding Sums up to 8

A. Practice addition up to 4 + 4.

4 + 2 = 6   3 + 3 = 6
4 + 4 = 8   4 + 3 = 7
3 + 4 = 7   3 + 2 = 5
2 + 3 = 5   2 + 4 = 6
4 + 1 = 5   3 + 4 = 7
2 + 2 = 4   0 + 4 = 4

B. Let's practice with some more difficult problems. Can you fill in the blanks?

2 + [3] = 5   [7] + 1 = 8
[2] + 2 = 4   [4] + 3 = 7
[3] + 4 = 7   4 + [4] = 8
6 + [1] = 7   [4] + 2 = 6
[1] + 2 = 3   4 + [0] = 4

Day 31

Counting Backwards

A. Follow the path from 20 to 1.

20	19	13	7	1	12	15	2	9
4	14	18	6	18	11	17	5	6
10	16	17	9	7	3	7	6	5	4
3	15	[ ]	11	10	9	8	19	4	3
16	14	13	12	1	8	16	12	1	2
2	17	11	13	5	10	15	8	Finish

B. Count backwards from 20 to 1. Try not to look at the path above.

20   16 15 14
19 18 17   13 12 11 10
                        9
1 2 3 4 5 6 7 8

Day 32

Adding Sums up to 7 & Counting by 10s

A. Practice addition up to 5 + 2 and 2 + 5.

5 +2 = 7	2 +3 = 5	4 +2 = 6	5 +1 = 6	2 +4 = 6	2 +2 = 4	2 +5 = 7	3 +2 = 5
2 +5 = 7	1 +3 = 4	2 +4 = 6	3 +2 = 5	5 +2 = 7	2 +3 = 5	1 +4 = 5	4 +2 = 6

B. Count by 10s. Fill in the missing numbers.

10 20 30 40 50
40 50 60 70 80
60 70 80 90 100
30 40 50 60 70

Day 33

Adding Sums up to 8 & Counting by 10s

A. Practice addition up to 5 + 3 and 3 + 5.

5 +3 = 8	2 +4 = 6	5 +2 = 7	3 +3 = 6	4 +3 = 7	3 +2 = 5	3 +5 = 8	2 +2 = 4
3 +5 = 8	5 +1 = 6	2 +3 = 5	4 +0 = 4	2 +5 = 7	5 +3 = 8	4 +2 = 6	3 +4 = 7

B. Count backward by 10s. Fill in the missing numbers.

50 40 30 20 10
80 70 60 50 40
100 90 80 70 60
60 50 40 30 20

Day 34

Adding Sums up to 9 & Counting by 10s

A. Practice addition up to 4 + 5 and 5 + 4.

4 +5 = 9	5 +3 = 8	4 +4 = 8	3 +2 = 5	4 +2 = 6	2 +5 = 7	3 +3 = 6	5 +4 = 9
5 +4 = 9	3 +4 = 7	2 +2 = 4	4 +5 = 9	3 +3 = 6	5 +4 = 9	2 +5 = 7	4 +4 = 8

B. Count by 10s. Fill in the missing numbers.

10 20 30 40 50 60
40 50 60 70 80 90
50 60 70 80 90 100
20 30 40 50 60 70

Day 35

Adding Sums up to 10

Practice addition up to 5 + 5.

5 +5 = 10	5 +2 = 7	4 +4 = 8	4 +3 = 7	3 +5 = 8	4 +5 = 9		
5 +4 = 9	2 +5 = 7	3 +3 = 6	2 +4 = 6	5 +5 = 10	3 +5 = 8	5 +0 = 5	3 +4 = 7

1 + 8 = 9   1 + [6] = 7
2 + [5] = 7   3 + [2] = 5
1 + 2 = 3   1 + 0 = 1
4 + 4 = 8   4 + [2] = 6
0 + [6] = 6   7 + 1 = 8
5 + 4 = 9   5 + [5] = 10

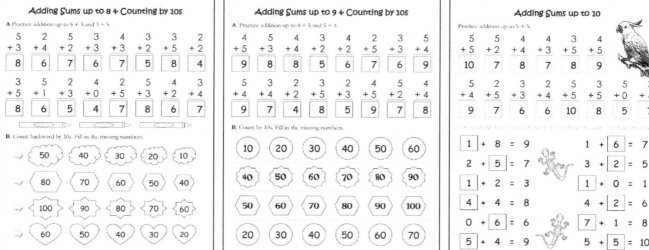

Day 36

Addition Practice

A. Solve the addition problems.

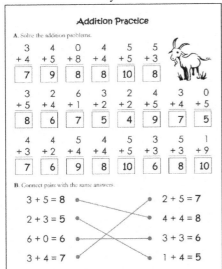

3	4	0	4	5	5
+4	+5	+8	+4	+5	+3
7	9	8	8	10	8

3	2	6	3	2	4	3	0
+5	+4	+1	+2	+2	+5	+4	+5
8	6	7	5	4	9	7	5

4	4	5	4	5	3	5	1
+3	+2	+4	+4	+5	+3	+3	+9
7	6	9	8	10	6	8	10

B. Connect pairs with the same answers.

3 + 5 = 8   2 + 5 = 7
2 + 3 = 5   4 + 4 = 8
6 + 0 = 6   3 + 3 = 6
3 + 4 = 7   1 + 4 = 5

Day 37

Addition Practice

A. Solve the addition problems.

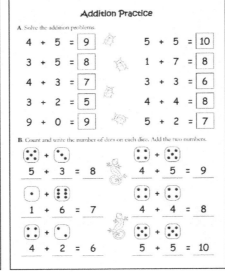

4 + 5 = 9   5 + 5 = 10
3 + 5 = 8   1 + 7 = 8
4 + 3 = 7   3 + 3 = 6
3 + 2 = 5   4 + 4 = 8
9 + 0 = 9   5 + 2 = 7

B. Count and write the number of dots on each dice. Add the two numbers.

5 + 3 = 8   4 + 5 = 9
1 + 6 = 7   4 + 4 = 8
4 + 2 = 6   5 + 5 = 10

Day 38

Addition Practice

A. Solve the addition problems.

5	2	3	1	9	5	4	4
+4	+3	+5	+8	+0	+2	+4	+2
9	5	8	9	9	7	8	6

3 + 4 = 7   4 + 5 = 9
1 + 9 = 10   5 + 5 = 10
2 + 5 = 7   8 + 0 = 8

B. Fill in the missing numbers.

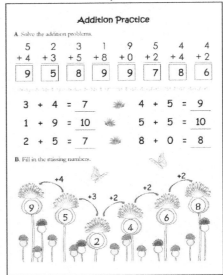

9 → 5 (+4) → ... (+3) → 2 (+2) → 4 (+2) → 6 (+2) → 8

Day 39

Addition Practice

A. Solve the addition problems.

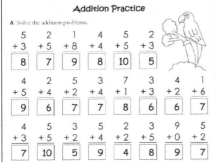

5	2	1	4	5	2
+3	+5	+8	+4	+5	+3
8	7	9	8	10	5

4	2	5	3	7	3	4	1
+5	+4	+2	+4	+1	+3	+2	+6
9	6	7	7	8	6	6	7

4	5	3	5	2	3	9	5
+3	+5	+2	+4	+2	+5	+0	+2
7	10	5	9	4	8	9	7

B. Solve the addition problems.

2 + 3 = 5, + 2 = 4
1 + 4 = 5, + 3 = 7
5 + 3 = 8, + 3 = 4... 7   8

Day 40

Addition Maze

Add your way through the maze to lead the fish to its friend.

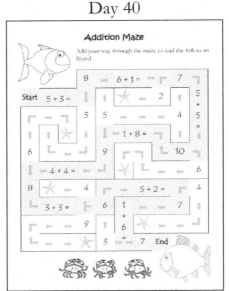

Start 5 + 3 =
6 + 1 =
1 + 8 =
4 + 4 =
5 + 2 =
3 + 3 =
End

Day 41

Addition Practice

Solve the addition problems.

1. 5 + 4 = 9
2. 3 + 1 = 4
3. 2 + 4 = 6
4. 8 + 0 = 8
5. 1 + 2 = 3
6. 7 + 1 = 8
7. 0 + 6 = 6
8. 5 + 3 = 8
9. 3 + 2 = 5
10. 3 + 5 = 8
11. 4 + 4 = 8
12. 8 + 1 = 9
13. 3 + 4 = 7
14. 2 + 2 = 4
15. 4 + 3 = 7
16. 5 + 5 = 10
17. 1 + 3 = 4
18. 5 + 2 = 7
19. 3 + 3 = 6
20. 2 + 5 = 7

Day 42

Odd or Even

A. Circle the pictures with an odd number. Remember that odd numbers end in 1, 3, 5, 7, or 9.

45   84   26   17
36   71   50   51

B. Color all the even-numbered leaves. Even numbers end in 2, 4, 6, 8, or 0.

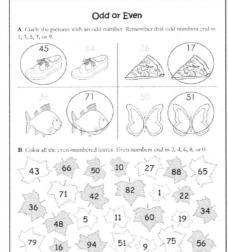

43 66 50 10 27 88 65
71 42 82 1 22
36 48 5 11 60 19 34
79 16 94 51 75 56

Day 43

Ordinals & Addition

Use the following drawing to complete the worksheet.

A. Color the **fourth**, **sixth** and **tenth** shapes.

B. Write the positions of each shape.

♡ first fourth seventh   ⬠ sixth eighth
☆ second third ninth tenth   ◇ fifth

C. Count each shape and write it as a number and a number word.

♡ 3 three   ⬠ 2 two
☆ 4 four   ◇ 1 one

D. Count and write the number of each shape. Add the two numbers.

3 + 2 = 5   4 + 3 = 7
4 + 1 = 5   1 + 2 = 3

Day 44

Ordinals & Addition

A. Color the **second**, **fifth** and **ninth** shapes. Draw X over the **first** shape.

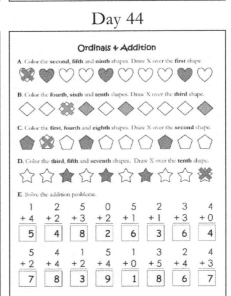

B. Color the **fourth**, **sixth** and **tenth** shapes. Draw X over the **third** shape.

C. Color the **first**, **fourth** and **eighth** shapes. Draw X over the **second** shape.

D. Color the **third**, **fifth** and **seventh** shapes. Draw X over the **tenth** shape.

E. Solve the addition problems.

1	5	0	5	2	3	4
+4	+2	+3	+2	+1	+1	+0
5	4	8	2	6	3	4

5	4	1	5	1	2	4
+2	+4	+2	+4	+0	+5	+3
7	8	3	9	1	6	7

Day 45

Counting by 10s

A. Color in the blocks as you count by 10s.

10	ten
20	twenty
30	thirty
40	forty
50	fifty
60	sixty
70	seventy
80	eighty
90	ninety
100	one hundred

B. Count backward by 10s. Fill in the missing numbers.

100 90 80 ☐ ☐ 30 20 10
  70 60 50 40

Day 46+

Daily Practice for the Week

From **Day 46** to **Day 50**, solve one row of problems each day.

3 +3 **6**	3 +2 **5**	4 +5 **9**	5 +3 **8**	8 +1 **9**	4 +2 **6**	5 +5 **10**	4 +4 **8**
2 +3 **5**	5 +2 **7**	5 +5 **10**	4 +3 **7**	9 +0 **9**	2 +4 **6**	2 +2 **4**	4 +3 **7**
5 +4 **9**	3 +2 **5**	1 +7 **8**	4 +2 **6**	3 +4 **7**	2 +5 **7**	3 +3 **6**	5 +5 **10**
3 +5 **8**	2 +4 **6**	4 +3 **7**	5 +5 **10**	7 +0 **7**	4 +5 **9**	3 +2 **5**	9 +1 **10**
2 +2 **4**	5 +5 **10**	4 +2 **6**	6 +1 **7**	3 +3 **6**	4 +4 **8**	2 +5 **7**	5 +4 **9**

Day 46

Shape Patterns

Draw the shape that comes next.

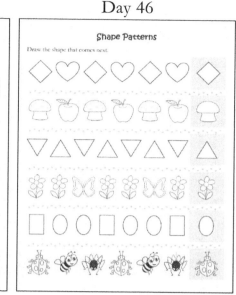

Day 47

Shape Patterns

Draw the missing shape to complete the pattern.

Day 48

Shape Patterns

Draw the missing shape to complete the pattern.

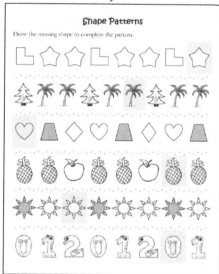

Day 49

Shape Patterns

Draw the missing shapes to complete the pattern.

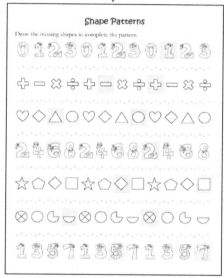

Day 50

Matching Patterns

Find the pattern that repeats the same way.

Pattern A	Pattern B
1 2 3 1 2 3	1 2 2 1 2 2

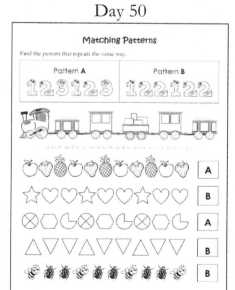

Day 51+

Daily Practice for the Week

From **Day 51** to **Day 55**, solve one row of problems each day.

5 +2 **7**	4 +4 **8**	5 +5 **10**	4 +2 **6**	2 +5 **7**	2 +3 **5**	3 +4 **7**	4 +5 **9**
2 +3 **5**	5 +3 **8**	2 +4 **6**	3 +3 **6**	5 +4 **9**	10 +0 **10**	5 +5 **10**	
3 +3 **6**	4 +5 **9**	3 +2 **5**	2 +2 **4**	9 +1 **10**	2 +3 **5**	2 +4 **6**	5 +2 **7**
4 +4 **8**	2 +5 **7**	5 +5 **10**	7 +0 **7**	4 +2 **6**	3 +4 **7**	4 +3 **7**	3 +5 **8**
2 +2 **4**	5 +4 **9**	3 +2 **5**	4 +4 **8**	3 +3 **6**	5 +5 **10**	2 +5 **7**	8 +1 **9**

Day 51

Comparing Numbers

A. For each pair, circle the picture with the larger number.

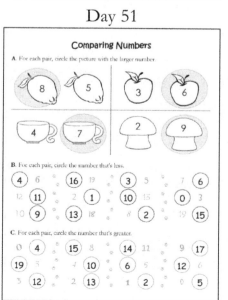

B. For each pair, circle the number that's less.

(4) 6   (16) 19   (3) 5   7 (6)
12 (11)   2 (1)   (10) 15   (0) 3
10 (9)   (13) 18   (2) 15   19 (15)

C. For each pair, circle the number that's greater.

0 (4)   (15) 8   (14) 11   9 (17)
(19) 5   (10) 4   (6) 5   (12) 6
5 (12)   2 (13)   1 (2)   2 (5)

Day 52

Comparing Numbers

A. Compare the numbers with < (less than), > (greater than), or = (equal to).

3 < 6	12 = 12	5 < 13
2 < 4	18 > 10	12 > 6
9 > 7	19 > 16	20 = 20
4 < 5	13 < 18	15 = 15
0 < 8	14 = 14	9 < 19
3 = 3	17 > 15	20 > 10
6 > 2	10 < 11	0 < 20

B. Write the numbers in order from smallest to biggest.

18, 3, 7, 12 → 3 7 12 18

6, 19, 2, 10 → 2 6 10 19

Day 53

Comparing Numbers

A. Compare the numbers with < (less than), > (greater than), or = (equal to).

3 < 6	22 < 28	20 < 31
2 > 1	43 > 41	42 = 42
9 > 7	15 < 17	37 > 27
0 < 8	50 = 50	15 < 48
5 > 4	33 < 34	40 > 39

B. Compare the sums with < (less than), > (greater than), or = (equal to).

3 + 3 < 2 + 5	3 + 5 = 5 + 3
4 + 5 > 2 + 2	1 + 4 < 2 + 5
2 + 1 < 1 + 4	5 + 5 > 1 + 5
5 + 2 < 0 + 8	0 + 2 = 1 + 1

Day 54

Comparing Numbers

A. Compare the numbers with < (less than), > (greater than), or = (equal to).

8 = 8	21 < 51	45 = 45
1 < 3	30 < 80	18 < 19
9 > 5	55 > 54	72 < 82
6 > 4	66 > 33	95 > 53

B. Compare the sums with < (less than), > (greater than), or = (equal to).

2 + 3 = 0 + 5	3 + 3 = 2 + 4
3 + 1 < 3 + 2	1 + 4 > 2 + 1
5 + 2 > 1 + 4	2 + 3 < 4 + 4
2 + 2 > 1 + 1	0 + 2 > 0 + 1
3 + 0 = 0 + 3	4 + 3 > 3 + 2

Day 55

Comparing Numbers

A. Compare the sums with < (less than), > (greater than), or = (equal to).

2 + 3 = 4 + 1	5 + 2 < 5 + 3
4 + 0 > 0 + 2	3 + 4 = 2 + 5
2 + 1 = 2 + 1	5 + 5 > 1 + 5
5 + 2 > 1 + 4	0 + 2 = 1 + 1
0 + 5 < 2 + 4	3 + 1 < 4 + 3
3 + 3 > 3 + 0	2 + 3 < 2 + 5
4 + 2 = 2 + 4	0 + 0 < 0 + 1

B. Write the numbers in order from smallest to biggest.

20, 89, 75, 16 → 16 20 75 89

93, 47, 32, 55 → 32 47 55 93

Day 56+

Daily Practice for the Week

From **Day 56** to **Day 60**, solve one row of problems each day.

3 +3	5 +5	4 +3	2 +4	8 +1	3 +2	5 +2	3 +5
6	10	7	6	9	5	7	8
9 +1	4 +2	3 +5	2 +5	0 +7	3 +3	4 +5	5 +5
10	6	8	7	7	6	9	10
6 +1	3 +3	5 +2	4 +4	3 +5	2 +3	4 +2	1 +3
7	6	7	8	8	5	6	4
3 +2	2 +4	5 +3	10 +0	3 +5	2 +5	5 +4	4 +3
5	6	8	10	8	7	9	7
3 +4	5 +5	4 +4	2 +2	1 +3	5 +2	4 +2	2 +3
7	10	8	4	4	7	6	5

Day 56

Measuring Length

Get your ruler. Measure the length of each object in centimeters.

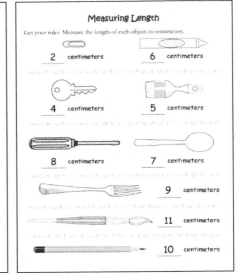

2 centimeters   6 centimeters

4 centimeters   5 centimeters

8 centimeters   7 centimeters

9 centimeters

11 centimeters

10 centimeters

Day 57

Measuring Length

Get your ruler. Measure the length of each object in inches.

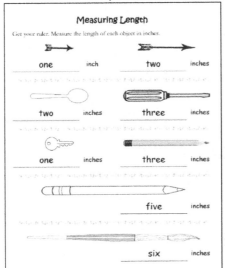

one inch   two inches

two inches   three inches

one inches   three inches

five inches

six inches

Day 58

Measuring Height

Color in the boxes to show how many units tall each animal is.

Day 59

Units of Measure

Which unit would you use? Circle the better unit of measure.

The length of a bus — (Feet) Inches

The distance between two cities — Yards (Miles)

The thickness of a math book — Yards (Inches)

The height of a building — (Feet) Miles

The length of a pencil — Feet (Inches)

The width of a playground — (Yards) Miles

Day 60

Addition Practice

A. Solve the addition problems.

1. 3 + 5 = 8
2. 1 + 2 = 3
3. 2 + 3 = 5
4. 4 + 5 = 9
5. 2 + 5 = 7
6. 4 + 2 = 6
7. 5 + 0 = 5
8. 3 + 1 = 4
9. 4 + 4 = 8
10. 2 + 2 = 4

B. Follow the numbers in the order of your answers above to help the turtle find its friend.

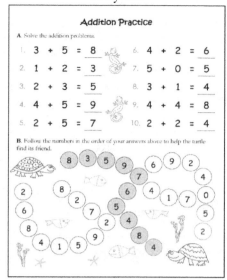

Day 61+

Daily Practice for the Week

From **Day 61** to **Day 65**, solve one row of problems each day.

3 +2	5 +5	3 +3	4 +4	1 +8	4 +5	5 +2	5 +3
5	10	6	8	9	9	7	8

4 +4	5 +2	3 +5	9 +1	2 +3	4 +3	2 +2	5 +4
8	7	8	10	5	7	4	9

4 +5	3 +4	0 +5	5 +5	4 +2	3 +2	2 +5	4 +4
9	7	5	10	6	5	7	8

5 +2	4 +4	5 +3	2 +3	10 +0	5 +4	4 +3	2 +4
7	8	8	5	10	9	7	6

5 +5	3 +2	4 +3	3 +5	3 +3	5 +2	2 +2	1 +7
10	5	7	8	6	7	4	8

Day 61

Addition Practice

A. Solve the addition problems.

5 + 4 = 9   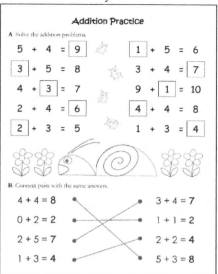   1 + 5 = 6

3 + 5 = 8   3 + 4 = 7

4 + 3 = 7   9 + 1 = 10

2 + 4 = 6   4 + 4 = 8

2 + 3 = 5   1 + 3 = 4

B. Connect pairs with the same answers.

4 + 4 = 8 ———— 3 + 4 = 7
0 + 2 = 2 ———— 1 + 1 = 2
2 + 5 = 7 ———— 2 + 2 = 4
1 + 3 = 4 ———— 5 + 3 = 8

Day 62

Reading Temperature

Write the temperature shown on each thermometer.

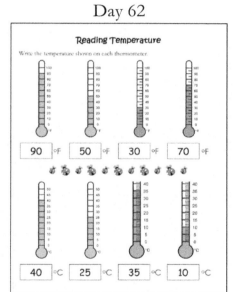

90 °F   50 °F   30 °F   70 °F

40 °C   25 °C   35 °C   10 °C

Day 63

Showing Temperature

Color the thermometers to show the correct temperature.

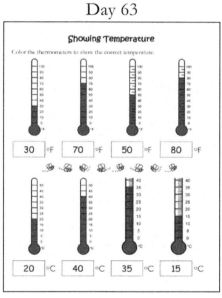

30 °F   70 °F   50 °F   80 °F

20 °C   40 °C   35 °C   15 °C

Day 64

Guessing Weight

Circle the lighter object.

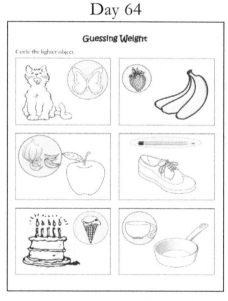

Day 65

Shape Patterns

A. Draw the missing shape to complete the pattern.

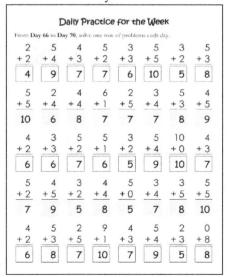

B. Count and write in the number of each shape. Add the two numbers.

(2) + 5 = 7   4 + (3) = 7

0 + (3) = 3   (2) + 4 = 6

(3) + 2 = 5   1 + (6) = 7

Day 66+

Daily Practice for the Week

From **Day 66** to **Day 70**, solve one row of problems each day.

2 +2	5 +4	4 +3	5 +2	3 +3	5 +5	3 +2	5 +3
4	9	7	7	6	10	5	8

5 +5	2 +4	4 +4	6 +1	2 +5	3 +4	5 +3	4 +5
10	6	8	7	7	7	8	9

4 +2	3 +3	5 +2	5 +1	3 +2	5 +4	10 +0	4 +3
6	6	7	6	5	9	10	7

5 +2	4 +5	3 +2	4 +4	5 +0	3 +4	3 +5	5 +5
7	9	5	8	5	7	8	10

4 +2	5 +3	2 +5	9 +1	4 +3	5 +4	2 +3	0 +8
6	8	7	10	7	9	5	8

Day 66

Comparing Numbers

A. For each pair, circle the picture with the larger number.

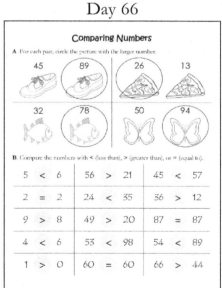

45   89   26   13

32   78   50   94

B. Compare the numbers with < (less than), > (greater than), or = (equal to).

5 < 6	56 > 21	45 < 57
2 = 2	24 < 35	36 > 12
9 > 8	49 > 20	87 = 87
4 < 6	53 < 98	54 < 89
1 > 0	60 = 60	66 > 44

Day 67

Odd or Even

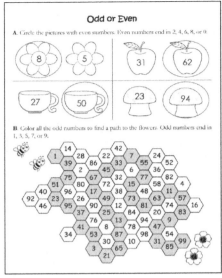

A. Circle the pictures with even numbers. Even numbers end in 2, 4, 6, 8, or 0.

8   5   31   62

27   50   23   94

B. Color all the odd numbers to find a path to the flowers. Odd numbers end in 1, 3, 5, 7, or 9.

Day 68

Ordinal Numbers

Draw lines to match the ordinal numbers.

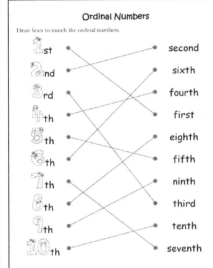

1st
2nd
3rd
4th
5th
6th
7th
8th
9th
10th

second
sixth
fourth
first
eighth
fifth
ninth
third
tenth
seventh

Day 69

Matching Patterns

Circle the pattern that matches the one on the left.

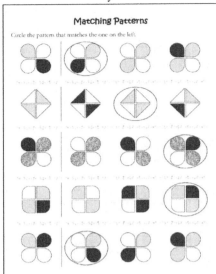

Day 70

Addition Practice

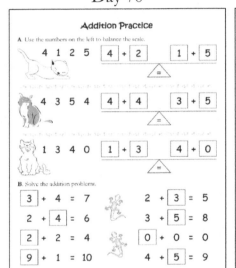

A. Use the numbers on the left to balance the scale.

4 1 2 5 | 4 | + | 2 | | 1 | + | 5 |
△ =

4 3 5 4 | 4 | + | 4 | | 3 | + | 5 |
△ =

1 3 4 0 | 1 | + | 3 | | 4 | + | 0 |
△ =

B. Solve the addition problems.

| 3 | + 4 = 7   2 + | 3 | = 5

2 + | 4 | = 6   3 + | 5 | = 8

| 2 | + 2 = 4 | 0 | + | 0 | = 0

9 + 1 = 10   4 + | 5 | = 9

Day 71+

Daily Practice for the Week

From **Day 71** to **Day 75**, solve one row of problems each day.

4	5	3	7	5	4	3	2
+3	+5	+4	+0	+3	+3	+2	+3
7	10	7	7	6	8	6	5

3	4	3	5	5	2	3	4
+1	+2	+5	+2	+4	+5	+2	+4
4	6	8	7	9	7	5	8

3	5	4	5	2	2	0	5
+3	+4	+3	+3	+3	+4	+4	+5
6	9	7	8	5	6	4	10

4	5	4	4	2	2	3	3
+1	+5	+4	+5	+5	+2	+5	+4
5	10	8	9	7	4	8	7

5	2	2	4	1	5	5	2
+4	+3	+4	+3	+6	+3	+5	+4
9	5	6	7	7	8	10	6

Day 71

Matching Shapes

Draw lines to match the shapes. Color each pair using the same color.

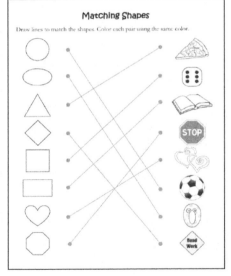

Day 72

Matching Shapes

Draw lines to match the shapes. Color each pair using the same color.

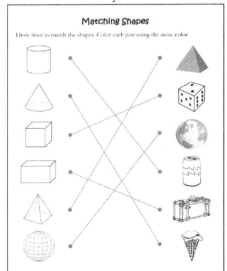

Day 73

Matching Shapes

A. Color each shape using different colors.

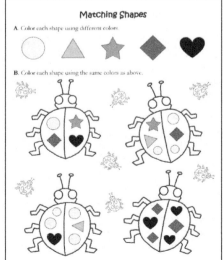

B. Color each shape using the same colors as above.

Day 74

Tangram Puzzles

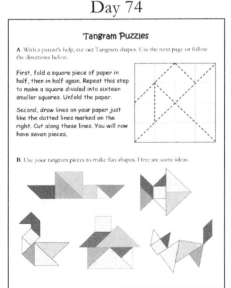

A. With a parent's help, cut out Tangram shapes. Use the next page or follow the directions below.

First, fold a square piece of paper in half, then in half again. Repeat this step to make a square divided into sixteen smaller squares. Unfold the paper.

Second, draw lines on your paper just like the dotted lines marked on the right. Cut along these lines. You will now have seven pieces.

B. Use your tangram pieces to make fun shapes. Here are some ideas.

Day 75

Geometric Shapes

Read aloud the name of each shape. Cover the names and see if you can remember them.

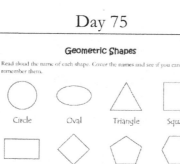

Circle	Oval	Triangle	Square
Rectangle	Diamond	Pentagon	Hexagon
Octagon	Star	Heart	Crescent
Sphere	Pyramid	Cube	Cone

Day 76+

Daily Practice for the Week

From **Day 76** to **Day 80**, solve one row of problems each day.

1 + 5 6	4 + 5 9	2 + 3 5	4 + 4 8	5 + 2 7	5 + 5 10	6 + 0 6	5 + 3 8
2 + 5 7	4 + 2 6	9 + 1 10	5 + 4 9	2 + 2 4	0 + 5 5	3 + 2 5	4 + 3 7
3 + 5 8	3 + 4 7	3 + 2 5	5 + 5 10	2 + 5 7	4 + 4 8	8 + 1 9	3 + 3 6
2 + 4 6	5 + 4 9	3 + 5 8	2 + 1 3	10 + 0 10	4 + 3 7	4 + 2 6	5 + 2 7
3 + 4 7	1 + 8 9	2 + 2 4	5 + 2 7	4 + 4 8	4 + 5 9	5 + 5 10	4 + 2 6

Day 76

2D Shapes

Match the 2-dimensional shapes to their names.

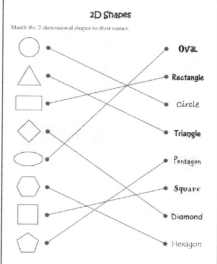

- Oval
- Rectangle
- Circle
- Triangle
- Pentagon
- Square
- Diamond
- Hexagon

Day 77

3D Shapes

Name and match the 3-dimensional shapes.

Sphere	Cylinder	Cone	Cube	Pyramid

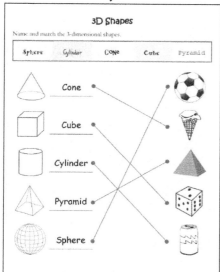

Cone
Cube
Cylinder
Pyramid
Sphere

Day 78

Shape Properties

A. Match the shapes, their names and properties.

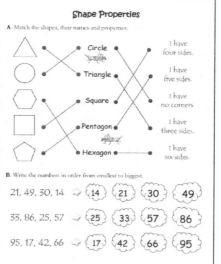

- Circle — I have four sides.
- Triangle — I have five sides.
- Square — I have no corners.
- Pentagon — I have three sides.
- Hexagon — I have six sides.

B. Write the numbers in order from smallest to biggest.

21, 49, 30, 14 → (14) (21) (30) (49)

33, 86, 25, 57 → (25) (33) (57) (86)

95, 17, 42, 66 → (17) (42) (66) (95)

Day 79

Counting Shapes

Count each shape in the picture. Don't miss the shape inside each flower!

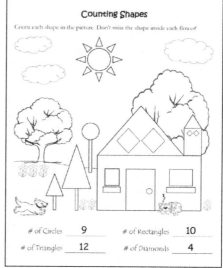

# of Circles	9	# of Rectangles	10
# of Triangles	12	# of Diamonds	4

Day 80

Identifying Shapes

Identify and color the correct shapes in each row.

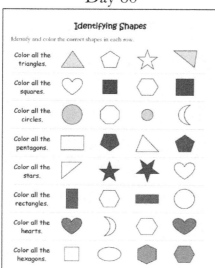

Color all the triangles.
Color all the squares.
Color all the circles.
Color all the pentagons.
Color all the stars.
Color all the rectangles.
Color all the hearts.
Color all the hexagons.

Day 81

Equal Parts & Addition

A. Draw X over the shapes that do not have equal parts. Then, circle the shapes that are divided in half with two equal parts.

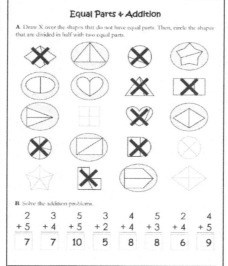

B. Solve the addition problems.

2 + 5 7	3 + 4 7	5 + 5 10	4 + 2 5	5 + 4 8	2 + 3 6	2 + 4 8	4 + 5 9

Day 82

Fourths & Addition

A. Circle the correct fraction of the shaded area.

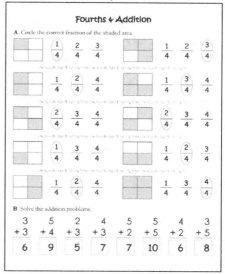

	$\frac{1}{4}$	$\frac{2}{4}$	$\frac{3}{4}$		$\frac{1}{4}$	$\frac{2}{4}$	$\frac{3}{4}$
	$\frac{1}{4}$	$\frac{2}{4}$	$\frac{4}{4}$		$\frac{1}{4}$	$\frac{3}{4}$	$\frac{4}{4}$
	$\frac{2}{4}$	$\frac{3}{4}$	$\frac{4}{4}$		$\frac{2}{4}$	$\frac{3}{4}$	$\frac{4}{4}$
	$\frac{1}{4}$	$\frac{3}{4}$	$\frac{4}{4}$		$\frac{1}{4}$	$\frac{2}{4}$	$\frac{3}{4}$
	$\frac{1}{4}$	$\frac{2}{4}$	$\frac{4}{4}$		$\frac{1}{4}$	$\frac{3}{4}$	$\frac{4}{4}$

B. Solve the addition problems.

3 + 3 6	5 + 4 9	2 + 3 5	4 + 3 7	5 + 2 7	5 + 5 10	4 + 2 6	3 + 5 8

Day 83

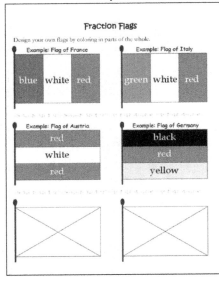

Fraction Flags

Design your own flags by coloring in parts of the whole.

Example: Flag of France
blue | white | red

Example: Flag of Italy
green | white | red

Example: Flag of Austria
red / white / red

Example: Flag of Germany
black / red / yellow

Day 84

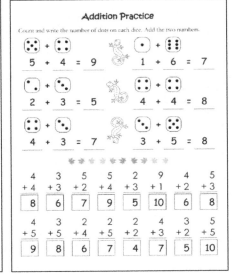

Addition Practice

Count and write the number of dots on each dice. Add the two numbers.

5 + 4 = 9

1 + 6 = 7

2 + 3 = 5

4 + 4 = 8

4 + 3 = 7

3 + 5 = 8

4	3	5	2	3	9	4	5
+4	+3	+2	+4	+3	+1	+2	+3
8	6	7	9	5	10	6	8

4	3	2	2	4	3	5
+5	+5	+4	+5	+3	+2	+5
9	8	6	7	4	7	5	10

Day 85

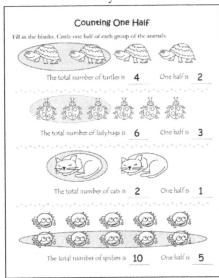

Counting One Half

Fill in the blanks. Circle one half of each group of the animals.

The total number of turtles is **4**   One half is **2**

The total number of ladybugs is **6**   One half is **3**

The total number of cats is **2**   One half is **1**

The total number of spiders is **10**   One half is **5**

Day 86

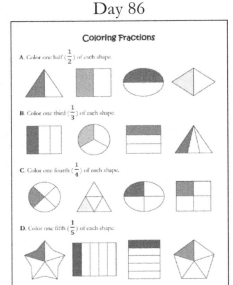

Coloring Fractions

A. Color one half ($\frac{1}{2}$) of each shape.

B. Color one third ($\frac{1}{3}$) of each shape.

C. Color one fourth ($\frac{1}{4}$) of each shape.

D. Color one fifth ($\frac{1}{5}$) of each shape.

Day 87

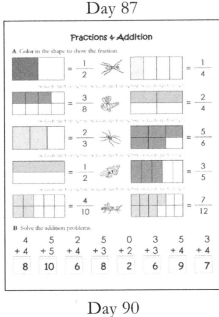

Fractions & Addition

A. Color in the shape to show the fraction.

= $\frac{1}{2}$ = $\frac{1}{4}$

= $\frac{3}{8}$ = $\frac{2}{4}$

= $\frac{2}{3}$ = $\frac{5}{6}$

= $\frac{1}{2}$ = $\frac{3}{5}$

= $\frac{4}{10}$ = $\frac{7}{12}$

B. Solve the addition problems.

4	5	2	5	0	3	5	3
+4	+5	+4	+3	+2	+3	+4	+4
8	10	6	8	2	6	9	7

Day 88

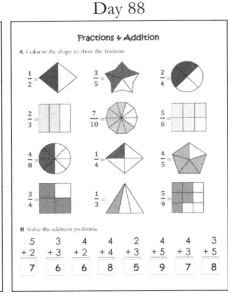

Fractions & Addition

A. Color in the shape to show the fraction.

$\frac{1}{2}$ = $\frac{3}{5}$ = $\frac{2}{4}$ =

$\frac{2}{3}$ = $\frac{7}{10}$ = $\frac{5}{6}$ =

$\frac{4}{8}$ = $\frac{1}{4}$ = $\frac{4}{5}$ =

$\frac{3}{4}$ = $\frac{1}{3}$ = $\frac{5}{9}$ =

B. Solve the addition problems.

5	3	4	4	2	4	4	3
+2	+3	+2	+4	+3	+5	+3	+5
7	6	6	8	5	9	7	8

Day 89

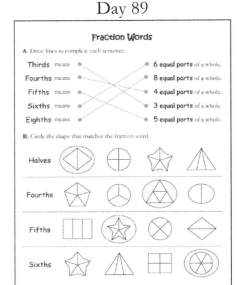

Fraction Words

A. Draw lines to complete each sentence.

Thirds means   6 equal parts of a whole.
Fourths means   8 equal parts of a whole.
Fifths means   4 equal parts of a whole.
Sixths means   3 equal parts of a whole.
Eighths means   5 equal parts of a whole.

B. Circle the shape that matches the fraction word.

Halves

Fourths

Fifths

Sixths

Day 90

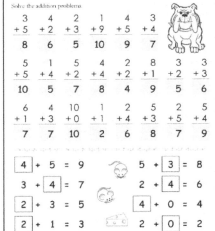

Addition Practice

Solve the addition problems.

3	4	2	1	4	3
+5	+2	+3	+9	+5	+4
8	6	5	10	9	7

5	1	5	4	2	8	3	3
+5	+4	+2	+4	+2	+1	+2	+3
10	5	7	8	4	9	5	6

6	4	10	1	2	5	2	5
+1	+3	+0	+1	+4	+3	+5	+4
7	7	10	2	6	8	7	9

4 + 5 = 9   5 + 3 = 8

3 + 4 = 7   2 + 4 = 6

2 + 3 = 5   4 + 0 = 4

2 + 1 = 3   2 + 0 = 2

Day 91

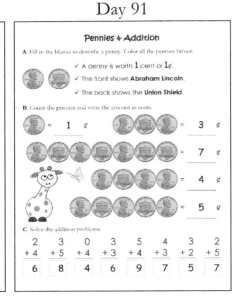

Pennies & Addition

A. Fill in the blanks to describe a penny. Color all the pennies brown.

✓ A penny is worth **1** cent or **1¢**.
✓ The front shows **Abraham Lincoln**.
✓ The back shows the **Union Shield**.

B. Count the pennies and write the amount in cents.

= **1** ¢   = **3** ¢

= **7** ¢

= **4** ¢

= **5** ¢

C. Solve the addition problems.

2	3	0	3	5	4	3	2
+4	+5	+4	+3	+4	+3	+2	+5
6	8	4	6	9	7	5	7

Day 92

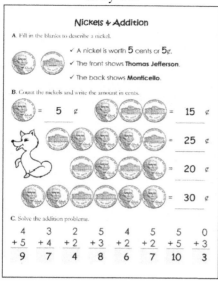

Nickels & Addition

A. Fill in the blanks to describe a nickel.

- ✓ A nickel is worth **5** cents or **5¢**.
- ✓ The front shows **Thomas Jefferson**.
- ✓ The back shows **Monticello**.

B. Count the nickels and write the amount in cents.

= **5** ¢

= **15** ¢

= **25** ¢

= **20** ¢

= **30** ¢

C. Solve the addition problems.

4	3	2	5	4	5	5	0
+5	+4	+2	+3	+2	+2	+5	+3
9	7	4	8	6	7	10	3

Day 93

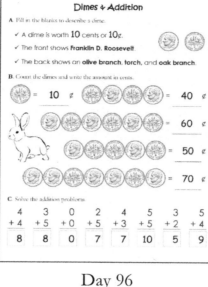

Dimes & Addition

A. Fill in the blanks to describe a dime.

- ✓ A dime is worth **10** cents or **10¢**.
- ✓ The front shows **Franklin D. Roosevelt**.
- ✓ The back shows an **olive branch, torch, and oak branch**.

B. Count the dimes and write the amount in cents.

= **10** ¢

= **40** ¢

= **60** ¢

= **50** ¢

= **70** ¢

C. Solve the addition problems.

4	3	0	2	4	5	3	5
+4	+5	+0	+5	+3	+5	+2	+4
8	8	0	7	7	10	5	9

Day 94

Nickels and Pennies

A. Find all the pennies and color them brown.

B. Count the nickels and pennies. Write the amount in cents.

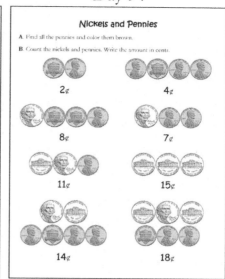

2¢

4¢

8¢

7¢

11¢

15¢

14¢

18¢

Day 95

Counting Backwards

A. Count backward out loud and fill in the missing numbers. Then, color the shapes with an even number. Even numbers end in 2, 4, 6, 8, or 0.

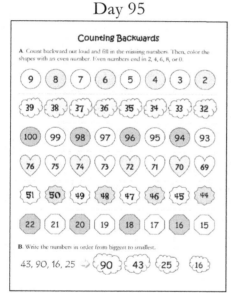

9	8	7	6	5	4	3	2
39	38	37	36	35	34	33	32
100	99	98	97	96	95	94	93
76	75	74	73	72	71	70	69
51	50	49	48	47	46	45	44
22	21	20	19	18	17	16	15

B. Write the numbers in order from biggest to smallest.

43, 90, 16, 25 → **90** **43** **25** **16**

Day 96

Dimes and Pennies

A. Find all the pennies and color them brown.

B. Count the dimes and pennies. Write the amount in cents.

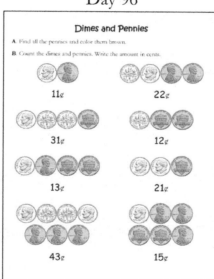

11¢

22¢

31¢

12¢

13¢

21¢

43¢

15¢

Day 97

Dimes and Nickels

Count the dimes and nickels. Write the amount in cents.

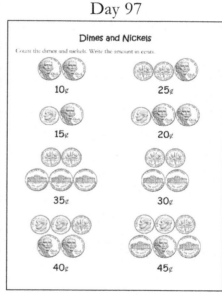

10¢

25¢

15¢

20¢

35¢

30¢

40¢

45¢

Day 98

Quarters

A. Fill in the blanks to describe a quarter.

- ✓ A quarter is worth **25** cents or **25¢**.
- ✓ The front shows **George Washington**.
- ✓ The back varies. The left image is a **Homestead National Monument of America** quarter for Nebraska.

B. Count the quarters and write the amount in cents.

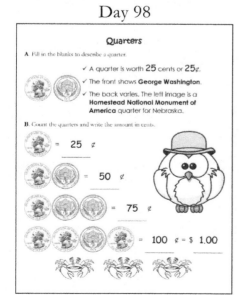

= **25** ¢

= **50** ¢

= **75** ¢

= **100** ¢ = $ **1.00**

Day 99

Identifying Coins

A. Find all the pennies and color them brown.

B. Match the picture, name, and value of the coins.

Dime — 5 cents

Quarter — 10 cents

Penny — 25 cents

Nickel — 1 cent

C. Match the front, back, and value of the coins.

— 5 cents

— 10 cents

— 1 cent

Day 100

Addition Practice

Solve the addition problems.

3 + 3 = **6**	3 + 4 = **7**
5 + 4 = **9**	4 + 2 = **6**
4 + 1 = **5**	0 + 8 = **8**
3 + 5 = **8**	5 + 2 = **7**
2 + 3 = **5**	4 + 4 = **8**

4 + 5 = 9	5 + **5** = 10
2 + **5** = 7	5 + **3** = 8
2 + 4 = 6	**2** + 1 = 3
3 + **2** = 5	4 + **3** = 7
9 + 1 = 10	**2** + 2 = 4

Day 101

Counting Coins

A. Find all the pennies and color them brown.

B. Count the coins. Write the amount in cents.

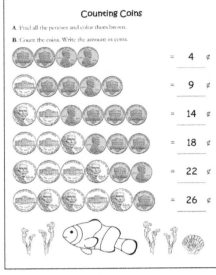

= 4 ¢

= 9 ¢

= 14 ¢

= 18 ¢

= 22 ¢

= 26 ¢

Day 102

Counting Coins

A. Find all the pennies and color them brown.

B. Count the coins. Write the amount in cents.

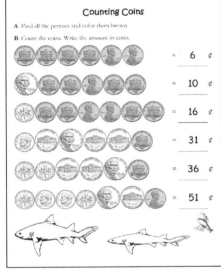

= 6 ¢

= 10 ¢

= 16 ¢

= 31 ¢

= 36 ¢

= 51 ¢

Day 103

Counting Coins

A. Find all the pennies and color them brown.

B. Count the coins. Write the amount in cents.

= 10 ¢

= 20 ¢

= 50 ¢

= 61 ¢

= 47 ¢

= 60 ¢

Day 104

Counting Coins

A. Find all the pennies and color them brown.

B. Which is worth more? Compare the amounts with >, <, or =.

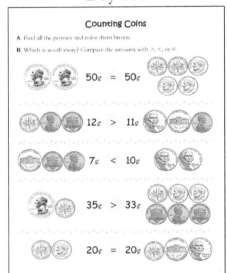

50¢ = 50¢

12¢ > 11¢

7¢ < 10¢

35¢ > 33¢

20¢ = 20¢

Day 105

Addition Practice

A. Solve the addition problems.

5 + 2 = 7   3 + 4 = 7
0 + 6 = 6   4 + 5 = 9
5 + 5 = 10   3 + 3 = 6
3 + 2 = 5   4 + 4 = 8
5 + 3 = 8   7 + 1 = 8

B. Color the cells with a sum that is an even number. Remember that even numbers end in 2, 4, 6, 8, or 0.

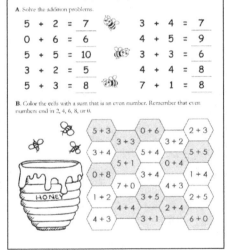

Day 106+

Daily Practice for the Week

From **Day 106** to **Day 110**, solve one row of problems each day.

2	3	5	4	4	5	3	3
+4	+4	+5	+4	+1	+5	+2	+2
6	7	10	8	6	9	7	5

1	10	3	2	4	2	4	5
+6	+0	+5	+2	+3	+3	+2	+4
7	10	8	4	7	5	6	9

4	3	4	7	3	4	5	5
+5	+2	+2	+1	+3	+4	+5	+3
9	5	6	8	6	8	10	8

3	5	4	3	3	2	2	9
+3	+2	+3	+2	+5	+5	+2	+1
6	7	7	5	8	7	4	10

5	4	5	1	2	2	5	4
+5	+2	+3	+1	+4	+3	+4	+4
10	6	8	2	6	5	9	8

Day 106

Coin Towers

A. Get out a handful of coins. Sort them into groups: all pennies into one group, all quarters into one group, and so on. Line the coins up on the table or floor to make one column per group. Draw your columns in the table below.

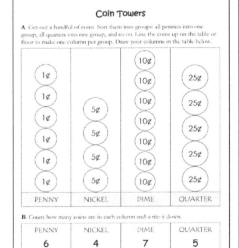

B. Count how many coins are in each column and write it down.

PENNY	NICKEL	DIME	QUARTER
6	4	7	5

Day 107

Coins Bar Graph

A. Get out a handful of coins. Sort them into groups. Count how many are in each group and write it down below.

PENNY	NICKEL	DIME	QUARTER
4	6	8	3

B. Draw towers for each group. For example, if you have four pennies, color in four blocks in the PENNY column. Use a different color for each group if you can. Write "Coin Count" at the top. This makes a **bar graph**.

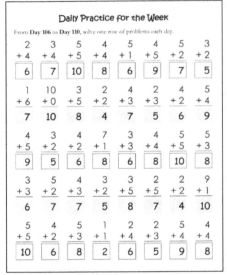

Day 108

My Graph Paper

Use this worksheet to practice graphing

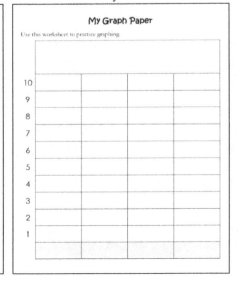

Day 109

Fruits Bar Graph

A. Count how many of each fruit there are.

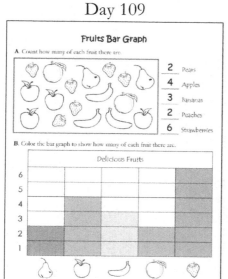

2	Pears
4	Apples
3	Bananas
2	Peaches
6	Strawberries

B. Color the bar graph to show how many of each fruit there are.

Delicious Fruits

Day 110

Addition Match

Draw lines to match the addition problems to their correct answers.

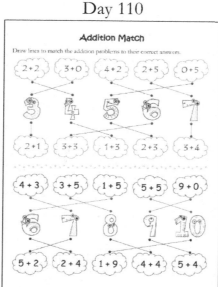

Day 111+

Daily Practice for the Week

From **Day 111** to **Day 115**, solve one row of problems each day.

4 + 3	5 + 5	5 + 3	2 + 5	4 + 4	3 + 3	2 + 3	9 + 1
7	**10**	**8**	**7**	**8**	**6**	**5**	**10**
4 + 5	2 + 4	1 + 6	2 + 2	4 + 2	3 + 4	5 + 2	3 + 5
9	**6**	**7**	**4**	**6**	**7**	**7**	**8**
3 + 3	4 + 4	2 + 3	4 + 3	2 + 5	0 + 9	5 + 4	1 + 5
6	**8**	**5**	**7**	**7**	**9**	**9**	**6**
1 + 1	4 + 5	4 + 2	5 + 3	3 + 4	2 + 2	5 + 5	5 + 2
2	**9**	**6**	**8**	**7**	**4**	**10**	**7**
3 + 5	0 + 4	2 + 5	3 + 2	7 + 1	2 + 3	5 + 4	3 + 3
8	**4**	**7**	**5**	**8**	**5**	**9**	**6**

Day 111

Bugs Pie Chart

Count how many bugs there are in each group. Color one slice for each bug, using the colors listed below.

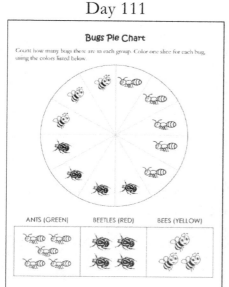

ANTS (GREEN)	BEETLES (RED)	BEES (YELLOW)

Day 112

Coins Pie Chart

B. Count how many of each coin there are.

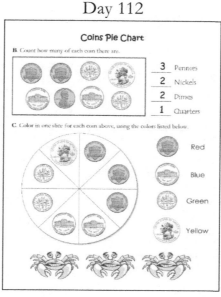

3	Pennies
2	Nickels
2	Dimes
1	Quarters

C. Color in one slice for each coin above, using the colors listed below.

Red

Blue

Green

Yellow

Day 113

Pets Picture Graph

The picture graph shows the pets your friends own. Use the graph to answer the questions.

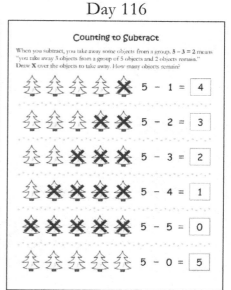

1. How many animals are there in total? **13**
2. How many dogs do your friends have? **3**
3. How many fish do your friends have? **2**
4. What kind of pet do your friends have the most of? **Cat**
5. What kind of pet do your friends have the least of? **Turtle**
6. Which pets are in a tie? **Dog** and **Bird**

Day 114

Pets Bar Graph

The bar graph shows the pets your friends own. Use the graph to answer the questions.

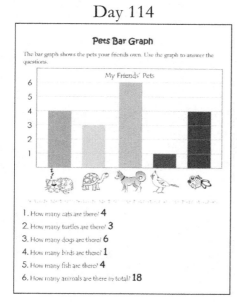

My Friends' Pets

1. How many cats are there? **4**
2. How many turtles are there? **3**
3. How many dogs are there? **6**
4. How many birds are there? **1**
5. How many fish are there? **4**
6. How many animals are there in total? **18**

Day 115

Graphing Zoo Animals

A. The pie chart shows the animals in the zoo. Count the number of each animal and fill in the blanks.

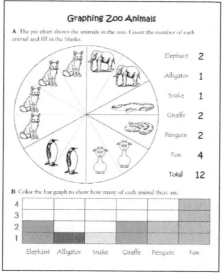

Elephant	**2**
Alligator	**1**
Snake	**1**
Giraffe	**2**
Penguin	**2**
Fox	**4**
Total	**12**

B. Color the bar graph to show how many of each animal there are.

Elephant	Alligator	Snake	Giraffe	Penguin	Fox

Day 116

Counting to Subtract

When you subtract, you take away some objects from a group. 5 − 3 = 2 means "you take away 3 objects from a group of 5 objects and 2 objects remain." Draw **X** over the objects to take away. How many objects remain?

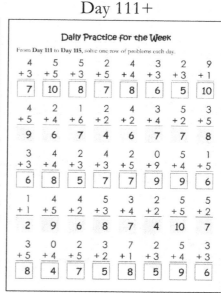

5 − 1 = **4**

5 − 2 = **3**

5 − 3 = **2**

5 − 4 = **1**

5 − 5 = **0**

5 − 0 = **5**

Day 117

Subtracting 1 on a Number Line

You can use a number line to subtract. Put your finger on 10. Jump one number to the left. That's subtracting one. Write the answer. Jump one more. Write the answer. Keep doing the same until you get to 0.

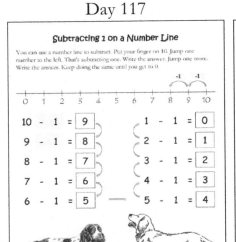

$$10 - 1 = 9 \qquad 1 - 1 = 0$$
$$9 - 1 = 8 \qquad 2 - 1 = 1$$
$$8 - 1 = 7 \qquad 3 - 1 = 2$$
$$7 - 1 = 6 \qquad 4 - 1 = 3$$
$$6 - 1 = 5 \qquad 5 - 1 = 4$$

Day 118

Subtracting 0 and 1

Let's practice subtracting 0 and 1

$3 - 0 = 3$	$7 - 1 = 6$
$6 - 1 = 5$	$5 - 0 = 5$
$2 - 1 = 1$	$3 - 1 = 2$
$1 - 0 = 1$	$6 - 0 = 6$
$4 - 0 = 4$	$4 - 1 = 3$
$8 - 1 = 7$	$2 - 0 = 2$
$7 - 0 = 7$	$1 - 1 = 0$

Day 119

Addition & Subtraction

A. Solve the subtraction problems.

4	3	4	2	5	1	3	2
-1	-0	-0	-1	-5	-1	-3	-0
3	3	4	1	0	0	0	2

5	3	2	4	1	5
-0	-1	-2	-4	-0	-1
5	2	0	0	1	4

B. Fill in the blanks to complete the addition and subtraction problems.

$8 - 8 = 0$	$4 + 3 = 7$
$5 + 5 = 10$	$6 - 0 = 6$
$2 + 4 = 6$	$2 + 2 = 4$
$1 - 0 = 1$	$4 + 5 = 9$
$2 + 5 = 7$	$3 + 2 = 5$
$4 + 4 = 8$	$9 - 1 = 8$

Day 120

Counting to Subtract

Draw X over the objects to subtract. Count the remaining objects.

$$5 - 1 = 4 \qquad 5 - 2 = 3$$
$$4 - 1 = 3 \qquad 4 - 2 = 2$$
$$3 - 1 = 2 \qquad 3 - 2 = 1$$
$$2 - 1 = 1 \qquad 2 - 2 = 0$$

Day 121

Add or Subtract?

Use the pictures to fill in the boxes with + (add) or − (subtract).

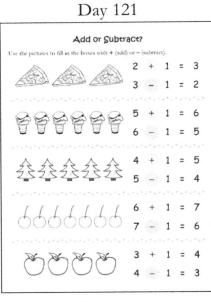

$$2 + 1 = 3$$
$$3 - 1 = 2$$
$$5 + 1 = 6$$
$$6 - 1 = 5$$
$$4 + 1 = 5$$
$$5 - 1 = 4$$
$$6 + 1 = 7$$
$$7 - 1 = 6$$
$$3 + 1 = 4$$
$$4 - 1 = 3$$

Day 122

Fractions & Subtraction

A. Circle the correct fraction of the shaded area.

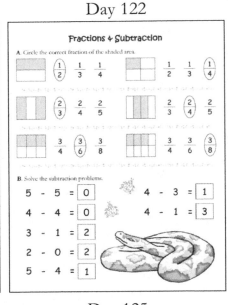

Row 1: ⭕$\frac{1}{2}$ $\frac{1}{3}$ $\frac{1}{4}$ | $\frac{1}{2}$ $\frac{1}{3}$ ⭕$\frac{1}{4}$

Row 2: ⭕$\frac{2}{3}$ $\frac{2}{4}$ $\frac{2}{5}$ | $\frac{2}{3}$ ⭕$\frac{2}{4}$ $\frac{2}{5}$

Row 3: $\frac{3}{4}$ ⭕$\frac{3}{6}$ $\frac{3}{8}$ | $\frac{3}{4}$ $\frac{3}{6}$ ⭕$\frac{3}{8}$

B. Solve the subtraction problems.

$$5 - 5 = 0 \qquad 4 - 3 = 1$$
$$4 - 4 = 0 \qquad 4 - 1 = 3$$
$$3 - 1 = 2$$
$$2 - 0 = 2$$
$$5 - 4 = 1$$

Day 123

Counting to Subtract

Draw X over the objects to subtract. Count the remaining objects.

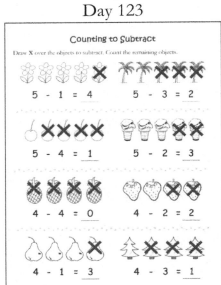

$$5 - 1 = 4 \qquad 5 - 3 = 2$$
$$5 - 4 = 1 \qquad 5 - 2 = 3$$
$$4 - 4 = 0 \qquad 4 - 2 = 2$$
$$4 - 1 = 3 \qquad 4 - 3 = 1$$

Day 124

Fractions & Subtraction

A. Color in the shape to show the fraction.

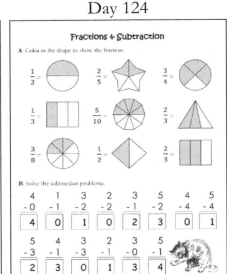

$\frac{1}{2}$ $\frac{2}{5}$ $\frac{3}{4}$

$\frac{1}{3}$ $\frac{5}{10}$ $\frac{2}{3}$

$\frac{3}{8}$ $\frac{1}{2}$ $\frac{2}{3}$

B. Solve the subtraction problems.

4	1	3	2	3	5	4	5
-0	-1	-2	-2	-1	-2	-4	-4
4	0	1	0	2	3	0	1

5	4	3	2	3			
-3	-1	-3	-1	-0			
2	3	0	1	3		4	

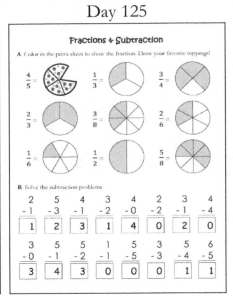

Day 125

Fractions & Subtraction

A. Color in the pizza slices to show the fraction. Draw your favorite toppings!

$\frac{4}{5}$ $\frac{1}{3}$ $\frac{3}{4}$

$\frac{2}{3}$ $\frac{3}{8}$ $\frac{2}{6}$

$\frac{1}{6}$ $\frac{1}{2}$ $\frac{5}{8}$

B. Solve the subtraction problems.

2	4	3	4	2	3	4
-1	-3	-1	-2	-0	-2	-1	-4
1	2	3	1	4	0	2	0

3	5	5	1	5	3	6
-0	-1	-2	-1	-5	-4	-5
3	4	3	0	0	1	1

Day 126

Fact Families

A **fact family** is a group of three numbers which combine to create two addition facts and two subtraction facts. Write the facts for each fact family.

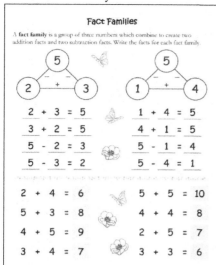

5 : 2 + 3

5 : 1 + 4

2 + 3 = 5
3 + 2 = 5
5 - 2 = 3
5 - 3 = 2

1 + 4 = 5
4 + 1 = 5
5 - 1 = 4
5 - 4 = 1

2 + 4 = 6
5 + 3 = 8
4 + 5 = 9
3 + 4 = 7

5 + 5 = 10
4 + 4 = 8
2 + 5 = 7
3 + 3 = 6

Day 127

Fact Families

Some fact families have only two facts: one addition fact and one subtraction fact. One example is a fact family for 3, 3, 6. Write the facts for each fact family.

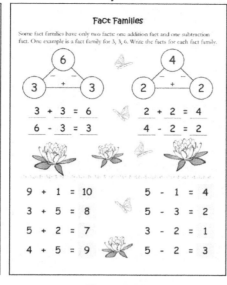

6 : 3 + 3

4 : 2 + 2

3 + 3 = 6
6 - 3 = 3

2 + 2 = 4
4 - 2 = 2

9 + 1 = 10
3 + 5 = 8
5 + 2 = 7
4 + 5 = 9

5 - 1 = 4
5 - 3 = 2
3 - 2 = 1
5 - 2 = 3

Day 128

Fact Families

Write the facts for each fact family.

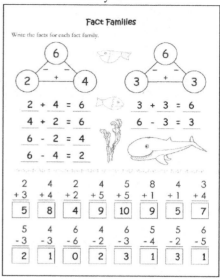

6 : 2 + 4

6 : 3 + 3

2 + 4 = 6
4 + 2 = 6
6 - 2 = 4
6 - 4 = 2

3 + 3 = 6
6 - 3 = 3

2	4	2	4	5	8	4	3
+3	+4	+2	+5	+5	+1	+1	+4
5	8	4	9	10	9	5	7

5	4	6	4	6	5	5	6
-3	-3	-6	-2	-3	-4	-2	-5
2	1	0	2	3	1	3	1

Day 129

Fact Families

Write the facts for each fact family.

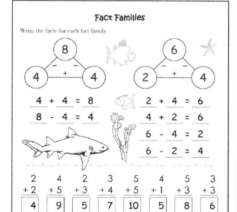

8 : 4 + 4

6 : 2 + 4

4 + 4 = 8
8 - 4 = 4

2 + 4 = 6
4 + 2 = 6
6 - 4 = 2
6 - 2 = 4

2	4	2	3	5	4	5	3
+2	+5	+3	+4	+5	+1	+3	+3
4	9	5	7	10	5	8	6

5	9	4	5	6	8	5	6
-2	-1	-2	-3	-5	-8	-4	-3
3	8	2	2	1	0	1	3

Day 130

Fact Families

Write the facts for each fact family.

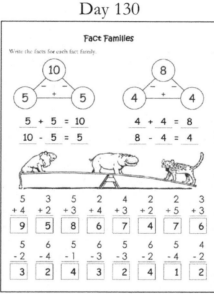

10 : 5 + 5

8 : 4 + 4

5 + 5 = 10
10 - 5 = 5

4 + 4 = 8
8 - 4 = 4

5	3	5	2	4	2	2	3
+4	+2	+3	+4	+3	+2	+5	+3
9	5	8	6	7	4	7	6

5	6	5	6	5	6	5	4
-2	-4	-1	-3	-3	-2	-4	-2
3	2	4	3	2	4	1	2

Day 131

Subtraction Practice

A. Solve the subtraction problems.

1. 6 - 3 = 3
2. 9 - 1 = 8
3. 5 - 3 = 2
4. 6 - 2 = 4
5. 10 - 5 = 5
6. 5 - 4 = 1

7. 8 - 4 = 4
8. 5 - 2 = 3
9. 6 - 4 = 2
10. 5 - 0 = 5
11. 4 - 2 = 2
12. 3 - 3 = 0

B. Follow the numbers in the order of your answers above to help the gecko find its friend.

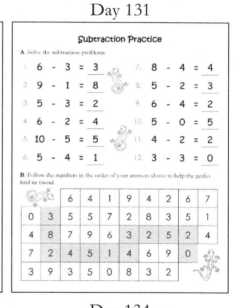

	6	4	1	9	4	2	6	7
0	3	5	5	7	2	8	3	5	1
4	8	7	9	6	3	2	5	2	4
7	2	4	5	1	4	6	9	0	
3	9	3	5	0	8	3	2		

Day 132

Fact Families

Write the facts for each fact family.

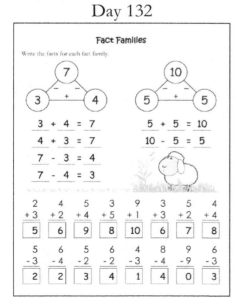

7 : 3 + 4

10 : 5 + 5

3 + 4 = 7
4 + 3 = 7
7 - 3 = 4
7 - 4 = 3

5 + 5 = 10
10 - 5 = 5

2	4	5	3	9	3	5	4
+3	+2	+4	+5	+1	+3	+2	+4
5	6	9	8	10	6	7	8

5	6	5	6	4	8	9	6
-3	-4	-2	-2	-3	-4	-9	-3
2	2	3	4	1	4	0	3

Day 133

Fact Families

Write the facts for each fact family.

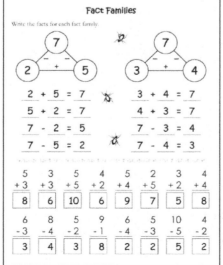

7 : 2 + 5

7 : 3 + 4

2 + 5 = 7
5 + 2 = 7
7 - 2 = 5
7 - 5 = 2

3 + 4 = 7
4 + 3 = 7
7 - 3 = 4
7 - 4 = 3

5	3	5	4	5	2	3	4
+3	+3	+5	+2	+4	+5	+2	+4
8	6	10	6	9	7	5	8

6	8	5	9	6	5	10	4
-3	-4	-2	-1	-4	-3	-5	-2
3	4	3	8	2	2	5	2

Day 134

Fact Families

Write the facts for each fact family.

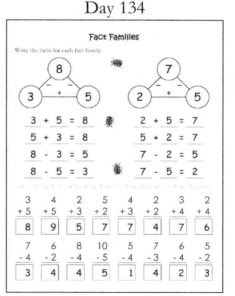

8 : 3 + 5

7 : 2 + 5

3 + 5 = 8
5 + 3 = 8
8 - 3 = 5
8 - 5 = 3

2 + 5 = 7
5 + 2 = 7
7 - 2 = 5
7 - 5 = 2

3	4	2	5	4	2	3	2
+5	+5	+3	+2	+3	+2	+4	+4
8	9	5	7	7	4	7	6

7	6	8	10	5	7	6	5
-4	-2	-4	-5	-4	-3	-4	-2
3	4	4	5	1	4	2	3

Day 135

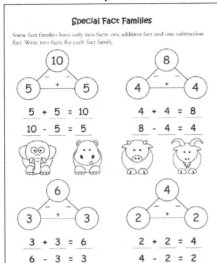

Special Fact Families

Some fact families have only two facts: one addition fact and one subtraction fact. Write two facts for each fact family.

10 / 5 + 5
5 + 5 = 10
10 - 5 = 5

8 / 4 + 4
4 + 4 = 8
8 - 4 = 4

6 / 3 - 3
3 + 3 = 6
6 - 3 = 3

4 / 2 - 2
2 + 2 = 4
4 - 2 = 2

Day 136

Counting to Subtract

Draw **X** over the objects to subtract. Read aloud the problem and answer.

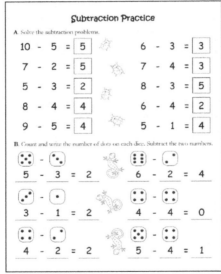

6 - 1 = 5	7 - 6 = 1	8 - 3 = 5
8 - 7 = 1	8 - 5 = 3	9 - 4 = 5
9 - 8 = 1	9 - 5 = 4	10 - 9 = 1

3 +3 = 6	2 +4 = 6	2 +3 = 5	5 +5 = 10	3 +4 = 7	3 +5 = 8	5 +2 = 7	4 +4 = 8

Day 137

Fact Families

Write the facts for each fact family.

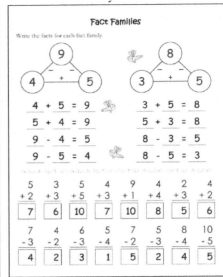

9 / 4 + 5
4 + 5 = 9
5 + 4 = 9
9 - 4 = 5
9 - 5 = 4

8 / 3 + 5
3 + 5 = 8
5 + 3 = 8
8 - 3 = 5
8 - 5 = 3

| 5 +2 = 7 | 3 +3 = 6 | 5 +5 = 10 | 4 +3 = 7 | 9 +1 = 10 | 4 +4 = 8 | 2 +3 = 5 | 4 +2 = 6 |

| 7 -3 = 4 | 4 -2 = 2 | 6 -3 = 3 | 5 -4 = 1 | 7 -2 = 5 | 5 -3 = 2 | 8 -4 = 4 | 10 -5 = 5 |

Day 138

Subtraction Maze

Subtract your way through the maze to lead the turtle to its friends.

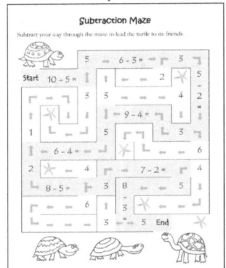

Day 139

Subtraction Practice

A. Solve the subtraction problems.

10 - 5 = 5   6 - 3 = 3
7 - 2 = 5   7 - 4 = 3
5 - 3 = 2   8 - 3 = 5
8 - 4 = 4   6 - 4 = 2
9 - 5 = 4   5 - 1 = 4

B. Count and write the number of dots on each dice. Subtract the two numbers.

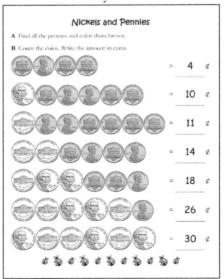

5 - 3 = 2   6 - 2 = 4
3 - 1 = 2   4 - 4 = 0
4 - 2 = 2   5 - 4 = 1

Day 140

Subtraction Practice

A. Solve the subtraction problems.

| 9 -9 = 0 | 8 -5 = 3 | 10 -5 = 5 | 7 -0 = 7 | 5 -4 = 1 | 3 -3 = 0 | 2 -1 = 1 | 6 -3 = 3 |

7 - 2 = 5   8 - 4 = 4
6 - 4 = 2   9 - 5 = 4
8 - 3 = 5   7 - 4 = 3

B. Fill in the missing numbers. Color the picture.

Day 141+

Daily Practice for the Week

From **Day 141** to **Day 145**, solve one row of problems each day.

| 6 -4 = 2 | 8 -5 = 3 | 5 -4 = 1 | 7 -2 = 5 | 4 -4 = 0 | 10 -5 = 5 | 9 -1 = 8 | 7 -3 = 4 |

| 5 +3 = 8 | 4 +4 = 8 | 2 +3 = 5 | 5 +5 = 10 | 4 +2 = 6 | 2 +5 = 7 | 3 +4 = 7 | 4 +5 = 9 |

| 5 -2 = 3 | 7 -5 = 2 | 9 -4 = 4 | 8 -0 = 8 | 7 -4 = 3 | 6 -3 = 3 | 5 -1 = 4 | 8 -3 = 5 |

| 3 +2 = 5 | 5 +4 = 9 | 3 +3 = 6 | 2 +2 = 4 | 5 +2 = 7 | 2 +4 = 6 | 3 +5 = 8 | 4 +3 = 7 |

| 10 -5 = 5 | 8 -4 = 4 | 5 -3 = 2 | 6 -2 = 4 | 9 -4 = 5 | 8 -5 = 3 | 4 -2 = 2 | 7 -2 = 5 |

Day 141

Nickels and Pennies

A. Find all the pennies and color them brown.

B. Count the coins. Write the amount in cents.

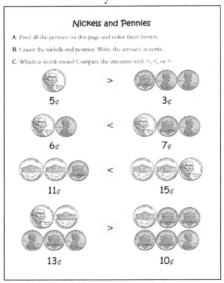

= 4 ¢
= 10 ¢
= 11 ¢
= 14 ¢
= 18 ¢
= 26 ¢
= 30 ¢

Day 142

Nickels and Pennies

A. Find all the pennies on this page and color them brown.

B. Count the nickels and pennies. Write the amount in cents.

C. Which is worth more? Compare the amounts with >, <, or =.

5¢ > 3¢

6¢ < 7¢

11¢ < 15¢

13¢ > 10¢

Day 143

Dimes

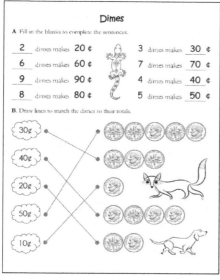

A. Fill in the blanks to complete the sentences.

2 dimes makes 20 ¢		3 dimes makes 30 ¢	
6 dimes makes 60 ¢		7 dimes makes 70 ¢	
9 dimes makes 90 ¢		4 dimes makes 40 ¢	
8 dimes makes 80 ¢		5 dimes makes 50 ¢	

B. Draw lines to match the dimes to their totals.

30¢ · 40¢ · 20¢ · 50¢ · 10¢

Day 144

Quarters

A. Fill in the blanks. Color the objects.

An apple costs 50¢. How many quarters do you need to buy it? — 2

A strawberry costs 25¢. How many quarters do you need to buy it? — 1

A muffin costs 75¢. How many quarters do you need to buy it? — 3

B. Draw lines to match the quarters to their totals.

50¢ · 25¢ · 100¢ · 75¢

Day 145

Counting Coins

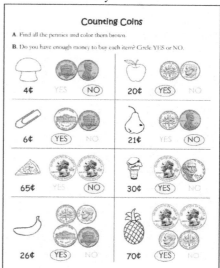

A. Find all the pennies and color them brown.

B. Do you have enough money to buy each item? Circle YES or NO.

4¢ YES (NO)		20¢ (YES) NO	
6¢ (YES) NO		21¢ YES (NO)	
65¢ YES (NO)		30¢ (YES) NO	
26¢ (YES) NO		70¢ (YES) NO	

Day 146+

Daily Practice for the Week

From **Day 146** to **Day 150**, solve one row of problems each day.

8 -4	6 -2	10 -5	6 -1	7 -2	9 -5	4 -2	7 -3
4	4	5	5	5	4	2	4
4 +4	6 +1	2 +4	2 +5	2 +2	5 +4	3 +2	5 +5
8	7	6	7	4	9	5	10
6 -3	5 -2	4 -3	8 -3	7 -4	8 -0	9 -4	6 -4
3	3	1	5	3	8	5	2
5 +3	3 +3	4 +2	2 +3	4 +5	4 +3	7 +1	1 +9
8	6	6	5	9	7	8	10
7 -5	6 -4	9 -5	5 -3	9 -1	7 -5	8 -3	10 -5
2	2	4	2	8	3	4	5

Day 146

Shapes Bar Graph

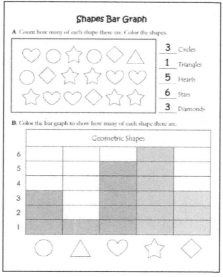

A. Count how many of each shape there are. Color the shapes.

3 Circles
1 Triangles
5 Hearts
6 Stars
3 Diamonds

B. Color the bar graph to show how many of each shape there are.

Geometric Shapes

Day 147

Shapes Pie Chart

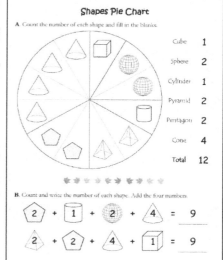

A. Count the number of each shape and fill in the blanks.

Cube	1
Sphere	2
Cylinder	1
Pyramid	2
Pentagon	2
Cone	4
Total	12

B. Count and write the number of each shape. Add the four numbers.

2 + 1 + 2 + 4 = 9

2 + 2 + 4 + 1 = 9

Day 148

Fraction Practice

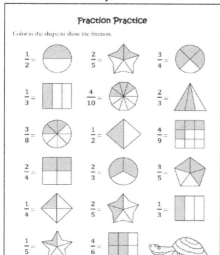

Color in the shape to show the fraction.

$\frac{1}{2}$ = $\frac{2}{5}$ = $\frac{3}{4}$ =

$\frac{1}{3}$ = $\frac{4}{10}$ = $\frac{2}{3}$ =

$\frac{3}{8}$ = $\frac{1}{2}$ = $\frac{4}{9}$ =

$\frac{2}{4}$ = $\frac{2}{3}$ = $\frac{3}{5}$ =

$\frac{1}{4}$ = $\frac{2}{5}$ = $\frac{1}{3}$ =

$\frac{1}{5}$ = $\frac{4}{6}$ =

Day 149

Fraction Practice

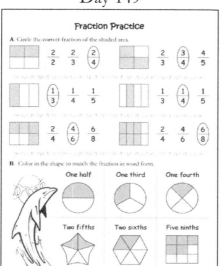

A. Circle the correct fraction of the shaded area.

$\frac{2}{2}$ $\frac{2}{3}$ $(\frac{2}{4})$ $\frac{2}{3}$ $(\frac{3}{4})$ $\frac{4}{5}$

$(\frac{1}{3})$ $\frac{1}{4}$ $\frac{1}{5}$ $\frac{1}{3}$ $(\frac{1}{4})$ $\frac{1}{5}$

$\frac{2}{4}$ $(\frac{4}{6})$ $\frac{6}{8}$ $\frac{2}{4}$ $\frac{4}{6}$ $(\frac{6}{8})$

B. Color in the shape to match the fraction in word form.

One half   One third   One fourth

Two fifths   Two sixths   Five ninths

Day 150

Subtraction Practice

Solve the subtraction problems.

5	- 2	3		7	- 3	4
3		2		4		2
2	- 1	1		3	- 1	2

9	- 5	4		6	- 2	4
4		3		3	
5	- 2	3		3	- 3	0

10	- 5	5		8	- 4	4
9	- 5	4		5	- 4	1

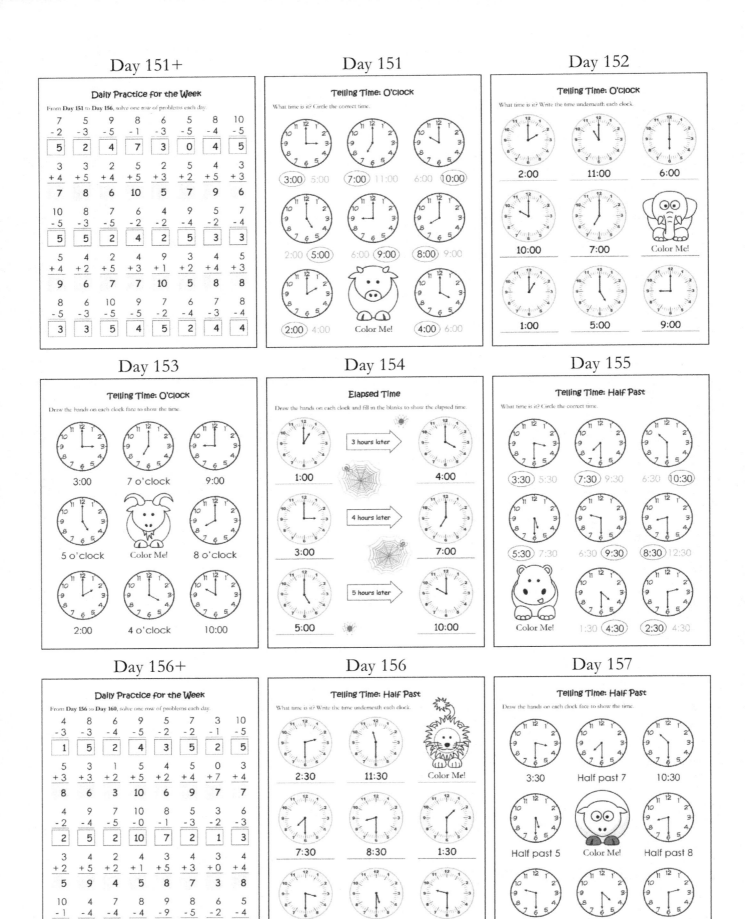

Day 151+

Daily Practice for the Week
From **Day 151** to **Day 156**, solve one row of problems each day.

7	5	9	8	6	5	8	10
- 2	- 3	- 5	- 1	- 3	- 5	- 4	- 5
5	**2**	**4**	**7**	**3**	**0**	**4**	**5**

3	3	2	5	2	5	4	3
+ 4	+ 5	+ 4	+ 5	+ 3	+ 2	+ 5	+ 3
7	8	6	10	5	7	9	6

10	8	7	6	4	9	5	7
- 5	- 3	- 5	- 2	- 2	- 4	- 2	- 4
5	**5**	**2**	**4**	**2**	**5**	**3**	**3**

5	4	2	4	9	3	4	5
+ 4	+ 2	+ 5	+ 3	+ 1	+ 2	+ 4	+ 3
9	6	7	7	10	5	8	8

8	6	10	9	7	6	7	8
- 5	- 3	- 5	- 5	- 2	- 4	- 3	- 4
3	**3**	**5**	**4**	**5**	**2**	**4**	**4**

Day 151

Telling Time: O'clock
What time is it? Circle the correct time.

(3:00) 5:00   (7:00) 11:00   6:00 (10:00)

2:00 (5:00)   6:00 (9:00)   (8:00) 9:00

(2:00) 4:00   Color Me!   (4:00) 6:00

Day 152

Telling Time: O'clock
What time is it? Write the time underneath each clock.

2:00   11:00   6:00

10:00   7:00   Color Me!

1:00   5:00   9:00

Day 153

Telling Time: O'clock
Draw the hands on each clock face to show the time.

3:00   7 o'clock   9:00

5 o'clock   Color Me!   8 o'clock

2:00   4 o'clock   10:00

Day 154

Elapsed Time
Draw the hands on each clock and fill in the blanks to show the elapsed time.

1:00   3 hours later   4:00

3:00   4 hours later   7:00

5:00   5 hours later   10:00

Day 155

Telling Time: Half Past
What time is it? Circle the correct time.

(3:30) 5:30   (7:30) 9:30   6:30 (10:30)

(5:30) 7:30   6:30 (9:30)   (8:30) 12:30

Color Me!   1:30 (4:30)   (2:30) 4:30

Day 156+

Daily Practice for the Week
From **Day 156** to **Day 160**, solve one row of problems each day.

4	8	6	9	5	7	3	10
- 3	- 3	- 4	- 5	- 2	- 2	- 1	- 5
1	**5**	**2**	**4**	**3**	**5**	**2**	**5**

5	3	1	5	4	5	0	3
+ 3	+ 3	+ 2	+ 5	+ 2	+ 4	+ 7	+ 4
8	6	3	10	6	9	7	7

4	9	7	10	8	5	3	6
- 2	- 4	- 5	- 0	- 1	- 3	- 2	- 3
2	**5**	**2**	**10**	**7**	**2**	**1**	**3**

3	4	2	4	3	4	3	4
+ 2	+ 5	+ 2	+ 1	+ 5	+ 3	+ 0	+ 4
5	9	4	5	8	7	3	8

10	4	7	8	9	8	6	5
- 1	- 4	- 4	- 4	- 9	- 5	- 2	- 4
9	**0**	**3**	**4**	**0**	**3**	**4**	**1**

Day 156

Telling Time: Half Past
What time is it? Write the time underneath each clock.

2:30   11:30   Color Me!

7:30   8:30   1:30

3:30   5:30   9:30

Day 157

Telling Time: Half Past
Draw the hands on each clock face to show the time.

3:30   Half past 7   10:30

Half past 5   Color Me!   Half past 8

9:30   Half past 4   2:30

Day 158

Elapsed Time

Draw the hands on each clock and fill in the blanks to show the elapsed time.

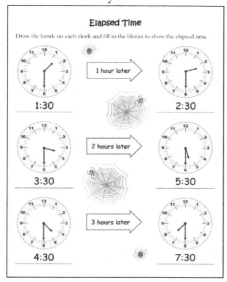

1:30   1 hour later   2:30

3:30   2 hours later   5:30

4:30   3 hours later   7:30

Day 159

Telling Time

Draw the hands on each clock face to show the time.

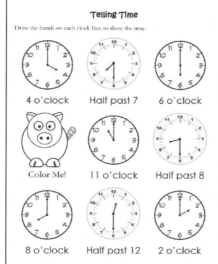

4 o'clock   Half past 7   6 o'clock

Color Me!   11 o'clock   Half past 8

8 o'clock   Half past 12   2 o'clock

Day 160

Telling Time

Draw the hands on each clock face to show the time.

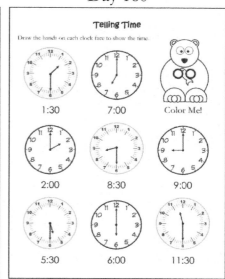

1:30   7:00   Color Me!

2:00   8:30   9:00

5:30   6:00   11:30

Day 161+

Daily Practice for the Week

From Day 161 to Day 165, complete one pattern each day and color it.

Day 161

Telling Time

Write the time underneath the clock or draw the hands on the clock face.

3:00   11:30   6:00

1:30   8:30   9:00

4:30   5:00   10:00

Day 162

Telling Time

Write the time underneath the clock or draw the hands on the clock face.

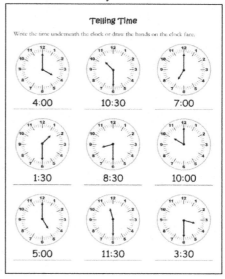

4:00   10:30   7:00

1:30   8:30   10:00

5:00   11:30   3:30

Day 163

Telling Time

Write the time underneath the clock or draw the hands on the clock face.

6:00   2:30   8:00

5:30   2:00   10:30

7:30   12:00   4:00

Day 164

Addition & Subtraction

A. Solve the addition and subtraction problems. Compare the answers with > (greater than), < (less than), or = (equal to).

5 + 5 = 10   >   9 - 1 = 8

4 - 3 = 1   <   2 + 3 = 5

2 + 5 = 7   =   3 + 4 = 7

5 + 4 = 9   >   4 + 2 = 6

8 - 4 = 4   =   7 - 3 = 4

B. Connect pairs with the same answers.

5 + 1 = 6   10 - 5 = 5
3 + 2 = 5   9 - 1 = 8
4 + 3 = 7   6 - 2 = 4
2 + 2 = 4   7 - 1 = 6
4 + 4 = 8   5 + 2 = 7

Day 165

Addition & Subtraction

A. Fill in the boxes with + (add) or − (subtract).

5 + 4 = 9   5 − 5 = 0

2 + 3 = 5   8 − 4 = 4

7 − 3 = 4   3 + 1 = 4

3 + 3 = 6   4 + 3 = 7

5 − 2 = 3   9 − 4 = 5

B. Connect pairs with the same answers.

7 - 3 = 4   5 + 0 = 5
3 + 2 = 5   3 + 3 = 6
2 + 5 = 7   8 - 1 = 7
4 + 2 = 6   4 + 4 = 8
0 + 8 = 8   9 - 5 = 4

Day 166

Time & Subtraction

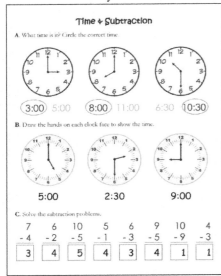

A. What time is it? Circle the correct time.

(3:00) 5:00   (8:00) 11:00   6:30 (10:30)

B. Draw the hands on each clock face to show the time.

5:00   2:30   9:00

C. Solve the subtraction problems.

7	6	10	5	6	9	10	4
-4	-2	-5	-1	-3	-5	-9	-3
3	4	5	4	3	4	1	1

Day 167

Time & Subtraction

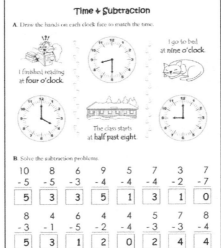

A. Draw the hands on each clock face to match the time.

I finished reading at four o'clock.

I go to bed at nine o'clock.

The class starts at half past eight.

B. Solve the subtraction problems.

10	8	6	9	5	7	3	7
-5	-5	-3	-4	-4	-2	-2	-7
5	3	3	5	1	3	1	0

8	4	6	4	4	5	7	8
-3	-1	-5	-2	-4	-3	-3	-4
5	3	1	2	0	2	4	4

Day 168

Money & Subtraction

A. Draw lines to match the same amounts.

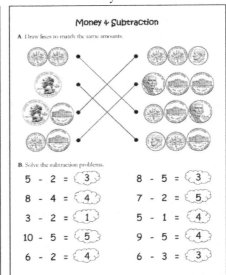

B. Solve the subtraction problems.

5 - 2 = 3   8 - 5 = 3
8 - 4 = 4   7 - 2 = 5
3 - 2 = 1   5 - 1 = 4
10 - 5 = 5   9 - 5 = 4
6 - 2 = 4   6 - 3 = 3

Day 169

Money & Subtraction

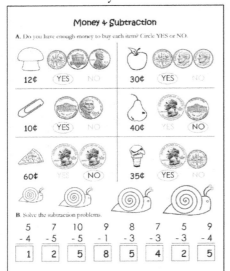

A. Do you have enough money to buy each item? Circle YES or NO.

12¢ (YES) NO   30¢ (YES) NO
10¢ (YES) NO   40¢ YES (NO)
60¢ YES (NO)   35¢ (YES) NO

B. Solve the subtraction problems.

5	7	10	9	8	7	8	9
-4	-5	-5	-1	-3	-3	-3	-4
1	2	5	8	5	4	2	5

Day 170

Addition & Subtraction

A. Solve the addition and subtraction problems.

1. 4 + 4 = 8   6. 3 - 2 = 1
2. 5 + 2 = 7   7. 5 - 3 = 2
3. 1 + 3 = 4   8. 8 - 4 = 4
4. 3 + 5 = 8   9. 9 - 5 = 4
5. 2 + 0 = 2   10. 6 - 3 = 3

B. Follow the numbers in the order of your answers above.

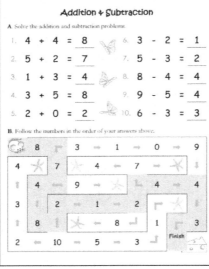

Day 171

Money Practice

Find all the pennies and color them brown. Then count the coins and write the amount in cents.

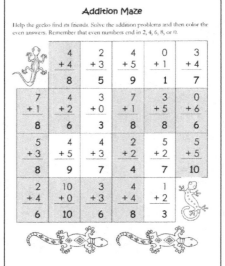

2¢   6¢   10¢
11¢   15¢   20¢
13¢   17¢   22¢
27¢   32¢   52¢

Day 172

Fraction Practice

A. Color in the circle to show the fraction.

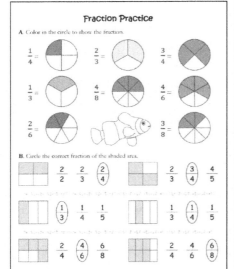

$\frac{1}{4}$ = $\frac{2}{3}$ = $\frac{3}{4}$ =

$\frac{1}{3}$ = $\frac{4}{8}$ = $\frac{4}{6}$ =

$\frac{2}{6}$ = $\frac{3}{8}$ =

B. Circle the correct fraction of the shaded area.

$\frac{2}{2}$ $\frac{2}{3}$ $(\frac{2}{4})$ $\frac{2}{3}$ $(\frac{3}{4})$ $\frac{4}{5}$

$(\frac{1}{3})$ $\frac{1}{4}$ $\frac{1}{5}$ $\frac{1}{3}$ $(\frac{1}{4})$ $\frac{1}{5}$

$\frac{2}{4}$ $(\frac{4}{6})$ $\frac{6}{8}$ $\frac{2}{4}$ $\frac{4}{6}$ $(\frac{6}{8})$

Day 173

Ordering Numbers

Write the numbers in order from smallest to biggest.

18, 1, 26, 95 → 1 18 26 95
53, 96, 21, 32 → 21 32 53 96
82, 13, 39, 74 → 13 39 74 82
33, 12, 93, 60 → 12 33 60 93
27, 6, 18, 53 → 6 18 27 53
81, 5, 58, 29 → 5 29 58 81
39, 0, 10, 45 → 0 10 39 45
11, 67, 32, 55 → 11 32 55 67

Day 174

Addition Maze

Help the gecko find its friends. Solve the addition problems and then color the even answers. Remember that even numbers end in 2, 4, 6, 8, or 0.

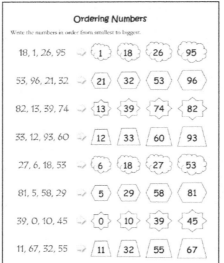

4 +4	2 +3	4 +5	0 +1	3 +4
8	5	9	1	7

7 +1	4 +2	3 +0	7 +1	3 +5	0 +6
8	6	3	8	8	6

5 +3	4 +5	4 +3	2 +2	5 +2	5 +5
8	9	7	4	7	10

2 +4	10 +0	3 +3	4 +4	1 +2
6	10	6	8	3

Day 175

Subtraction Maze

Help the turtle find its friends. Solve the subtraction problems and then color the odd answers. Remember that odd numbers end in 1, 3, 5, 7, or 9.

9 -4 = 5	7 -0 = 7	5 -2 = 3	7 -3 = 4	6 -2 = 4	8 -3 = 5
10 -1 = 9	6 -4 = 2	4 -1 = 3	10 -5 = 5	8 -4 = 4	7 -4 = 3
8 -7 = 1	5 -3 = 2	7 -5 = 2	6 -3 = 3	7 -2 = 5	8 -5 = 3

Day 176

Odd or Even

A. Write the number that comes before or after. Color in the **even** numbers.

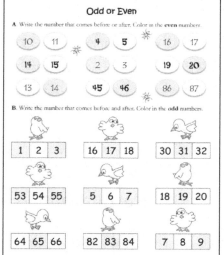

10	11		4	5		16	17
14	15		2	3		19	20
13	14		45	46		86	87

B. Write the number that comes before and after. Color in the **odd** numbers.

1 2 3	16 17 18	30 31 32
53 54 55	5 6 7	18 19 20
64 65 66	82 83 84	7 8 9

Day 177

Addition Match

Draw lines to match the addition problems to their correct answers.

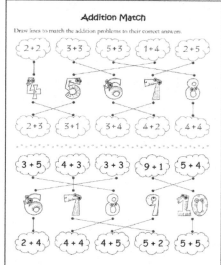

2 + 2   3 + 3   5 + 3   1 + 4   2 + 5

2 + 3   3 + 1   3 + 4   4 + 2   4 + 4

3 + 5   4 + 3   3 + 3   9 + 1   5 + 4

2 + 4   4 + 4   4 + 5   5 + 2   5 + 5

Day 178

Fact Families

Remember fact families? Fill in the circles.

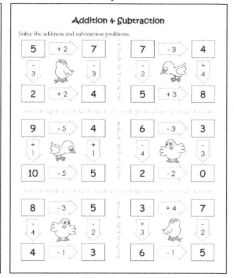

10   5 − + 5
9   4 − + 5
8   3 − + 5
8   4 − + 4
7   4 − + 3
7   2 − + 5
6   2 − + 4
5   3 − + 2

Day 179

Addition & Subtraction

Solve the addition and subtraction problems.

5 +2 7	7 -3 4
-3	-2
2 +2 4	5 +3 8

9 -5 4	6 -3 3
+1	-4
10 -5 5	2 -2 0

8 -3 5	3 +4 7
-4	+3
4 -1 3	6 -1 5

Day 180

Math Crossword

Solve the addition and subtraction problems.

4	+	3	=	7		8	+	1	=	9
-				-		-		+		-
2	+	2	=	4		5	+	0	=	5
=				=		=		=		=
2		6	-	3	=	3		1		4
		1		3	+	3	=	6		
		=				=		-		
10	-	5	=	5		2	+	4	=	6
-				=		=		=		
1	+	7	=	8		1	+	2	=	3
=										
9										

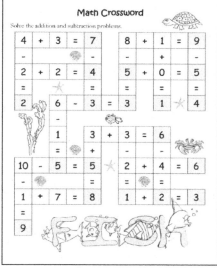

Congratulations!

You've completed first grade math!

We hope you had a great year with EP Math 1.

EP provides free, complete, high quality online homeschool curriculum for children around the world. Find more of our courses and resources on our site, allinonehomeschool.com.

If you prefer offline materials, consider Genesis Curriculum which takes a book of the Bible and turns it into daily lessons in science, social studies, and language arts for your children to learn all together. The curriculum also includes learning Biblical languages. Genesis Curriculum offers Rainbow Readers and a new math curriculum which is also done all together and is based on each day's Bible reading. GC Steps is an offline preschool and kindergarten program. Learn more about our expanding curriculum on our site, genesiscurriculum.com.

Made in the USA
Monee, IL
09 April 2020